Outdoing Jesus

OUTDOING JESUS

*Seven Ways to Live Out
the Promise of "Greater Than"*

Doug Pagitt

WILLIAM B. EERDMANS PUBLISHING COMPANY
GRAND RAPIDS, MICHIGAN

Wm. B. Eerdmans Publishing Co.
4035 Park East Court SE, Grand Rapids, Michigan 49546
www.eerdmans.com

25 24 23 22 21 20 19   1 2 3 4 5 6 7

ISBN 978-0-8028-7440-5

Library of Congress Cataloging-in-Publication Data

A catalog record for this book is available from the Library of Congress.

CONTENTS

CONTENTS

OUTDOING JESUS? REALLY?

The Centerpiece of Jesus's Message

1

We are all capable of miracles. Even Jesus-like miracles. You, me, all of us can do greater good works in our lives than Jesus did in his.

I know that might sound like a ridiculous or even sacrilegious claim. But that's exactly what Jesus intended.

This is really good news.

And it's happening all over the world, all the time.

The idea that we can do something greater than Jesus did isn't my idea. It's not even a new idea. Jesus states it quite clearly in John 14:12, "I assure you that whoever believes in me will do the works that I do. They will do even greater works than these because I am going to the Father."

Take a moment and let those two sentences settle in. If you want to double-check that they are actually from the Bible, I wouldn't hold it against you.

This teaching comes in the midst of a conversation Jesus has with his disciples about his impending death. He assures them that the works he has been doing will not come to an end; instead they will continue and even expand in the lives of those who follow in his ways. He encourages his disciples to understand this as a good thing.

I find this to be one of the most essential, provocative, and life-giving of all of Jesus's teachings. In fact, I believe it's the centerpiece of Jesus's spirituality and message.

The works to which Jesus is referring are the seven miraculous signs that make up the structure of John's Gospel. Maybe you're like me and you've heard these stories countless times over the years. Maybe they're new to you. Either way, I hope you'll consider this book an invitation to new ways of understanding these epic stories and what Jesus might be calling us to.

I read these miraculous signs as Jesus's wonderfully audacious call for humanity to do, and even outdo, his work, to be an ever-expanding benefit and blessing to all the world. They serve as a living framework leading us beyond tribal distinctions that pit one group of people against another; they lay out a way of life that implores us to leave behind fearful scarcity thinking, that frees us from oppressive systems, that brings an end to the fiction that the most powerful are those with the ability to control and to kill.

Jesus was a revolutionary invested in seeing humanity live up to its best, highest, most fulfilled, and God-infused potential (see Rom. 8:11). This empowering way of seeing the teaching of Jesus has significant impact on the shape of the communities and the religion that form around his life and teachings. If our faith calls us to create settings through which all people are invited to do even greater things than Jesus did, then it removes much of the competition and division between the sacred and the secular, the faithful and the not-so-faithful, the science-minded and the techno-skeptic. We become able to see all acts of goodness, technological advances, medical breakthroughs, and psychological discoveries and treatments as part of the same trajectory of healing, including, sharing, and resurrecting that Jesus was authorizing.

Jesus is calling us to drop our self-imposed limits and to follow the path he was on: to drink of the cup he drank from, to believe in God and to believe in him, to be "the salt of the earth" and "the light of the world" (Matt. 5:13–14), to take up our cross and follow him (Matt. 16:24).

When we see Jesus as the spark that started a fire warming the hearts of all people to demonstrate goodness, love, and inclusion, we begin to understand the Christian notion of incarnation not as the miraculous exception but as the magnificent rule—God in us and through us at all times and in all places.

We live in a spectacular world at an incredible time. By all measures, things have never been better for people than they are right now. I know that all is not right in the world. I know we're not even close to all the goodness that is necessary and possible. There remain countless ways people are held back by exclusion, violence, greed, sexism, exploitation, and the racism rooted in white supremacy. It's true that we continue to damage the planet in ways from which it may never recover. And we limit our imaginations in how we organize governments and economies, preventing far too many people from having long, healthy, fulfilled lives. Yes, we are still figuring out how to leave harmful and depressing narratives behind and embrace reconciliation, inclusion, nonviolence, generosity, equality, and sustainability.

But it remains true that there is less starvation, more education, fewer people living in poverty, fewer people enslaved by others, more people working, fewer wars and military conflicts, and more people deciding their own personal and national fates than at any other time in human history. And all of this is happening amid a growing world population.

We are on the verge of seeing even greater advances in every area of human life. I can't wait to introduce you to people who are making incredible strides in science, technology, philanthropy, and structural design; these people are bringing about changes in their fields that promote human flourishing and affect spiritual well-being—the agenda of God that Jesus was calling us to.

In this book, you'll meet ordinary people who have lived into the greater-than promise and are fulfilling the implications of this empowering, provocative, and encouraging message. They are making food available for a world population of more than seven billion people; they are engaging in collaborative work that brings peace to communities in conflict; they are developing new technologies in health and healing. These ordinary people are finding new ways to fund the needs of the underresourced around the world through entrepreneurship and philanthropy; they are making the earth more livable, acting with life-changing empathy, bringing back life when all hope seems lost, and saving the lives of the most vulnerable.

So has humanity outdone the works of Jesus?

I say the answer is yes. And that is just the way Jesus intended it to be.

NOT BETTER THAN, GREATER THAN

Entering the Jesus Path

2

I was raised in a family that didn't attend church or celebrate the religious elements of Christmas and Easter. We never read the Bible and we never prayed. My knowledge of Jesus was shaped by pop-culture references in movies, songs, and television. Needless to say, it was not a very well-formed knowledge. I didn't know anything about church, religion, or faith. And that was just fine with me; I had no sense that I was missing something.

My entrance on to the Jesus path was not compelled by a profound emptiness inside, nor did I sense that I was missing something, as is common in many conversion stories. What captured me was the riveting message of Jesus. It still captures me today. I think of myself—and all Christians—as called into a life as a follower of God in the way of Jesus. The message of Jesus captures that sense of being on the path, following in an active, engaged, meaningful way. I see myself moving along that long, beautiful, gracious path of life that Jesus walked and called people to. I too am invited to tread that path—or, as my friend Brian McLaren puts it, to "make the road as we travel."

It was this invitation to enter a path, a way of life and way of being, that drew me in as a sixteen-year-old. I had one of those personally transformative experiences that is common among people going through a spiritual awakening. It happened suddenly over a two-hour period while watching a passion play with a friend. What drew me deeply in was the story of Jesus declaring that God was on the side of humanity. To me, this drama captured the realities of life I knew to be true: just how hard life can be and how common it is to feel harassed by other people and to feel troubled by our own failures, doubts, and fears. The explicit imagery of Jesus on the side of people and Jesus declaring that God was on their side too was powerful for me.

I was, and still am, enamored with the idea that Jesus taught and modeled solidarity between God and humanity. This idea resonated with my deep knowledge that the connection between God and humanity is the default for all people in all situations without condition or qualification. Over the last thirty-five years, this has continued to draw me into living a life committed to that path and proclaiming "the greatest story ever told," the story of the partnership between God and humanity as seen in Jesus. We are called to do as Jesus did, to follow along that same path that Jesus followed, for the same reasons Jesus did, to tap into the fullness of our humanity and to share life with God.

I had a recent conversation about this with my friend Samir Selmanović, a spiritual teacher and life coach. He said, "It took me a while to recognize that I don't need to fear that all of our work is a threat to God. God doesn't have an ego problem. God is not worried about being outdone. To God, there is something more important than God. God is committed to the benefit and blessing of all humanity." In other words, "For God so loved the world that *he gave. . . .*"

Here is where the long-held understanding of Jesus as "the brother of humanity"—the one who is calling us all to live in the fullness of the family of God by doing and outdoing as an outflow of our shared humanity—is so powerful. It is an invitation to life, and one I accept as I attempt to organize my life and energies to empower the human spirit and foster life-giving community for a more beautiful, inclusive common good. This is the natural outflow of what it means for me, in my time, with my personality, with my passions and interests, to follow God in the way of Jesus as an act of faith.

Too Much Pressure?

The idea that Jesus was inviting all of humanity into a life made of goodness, God-ness, and to benefit and bless humanity is indeed good news. It's thrilling to know that we are not resigned to seeing Jesus as a far-off and far superior character whose goodness we are forced only to honor but never to perform. And when we hear that we not only will do those things but also are called to do and capable of doing even greater things, our hearts spring to life. I believe most people want to see the work we are doing in the world not as lesser goodness than that of our spiritual teacher, guide, and Lord, but as an extension of what he taught. And we certainly don't want the life of Jesus to be unapproachable or out of reach and thereby irrelevant to the places we work, the businesses we own, the people we love, the art we make, or the goodness we conspire to bring into reality.

We might find ourselves wanting to remake Jesus's statement into something more reasonable, like, "I assure you that whoever believes in me will do something significant, but in their own way, and while important to them, it is not really on the scale of what I accomplished. Sure, they will do great works, but only if graded on a curve with the 100 billion other people who have lived since the evolution of humans. They will do good, but not the kinds of things that rise to the level of a miracle."

But here's the thing: Jesus wouldn't make this command to do greater things if it were impossible to accomplish. No, Jesus said, my yoke is easy and my burden is light. That doesn't mean our efforts to do what Jesus did will always succeed. It doesn't mean hard things won't be demanded of us. But this call frees us from our limits. In other words, this is doable. And you are likely doing it already in your own particular way.

In the Way of . . .

My friend Luke Hillestad is an exceptional artist. In the coming decades, I expect the art world will hold him in the highest regard as a master painter. Luke studies with and in many ways emulates the work of his mentor, the famed Norwegian figurative painter Odd Nerdrum.

One of Luke's pieces hangs in my office. It is a big, bold painting with what people often refer to as a Rembrandt look to it. Almost everyone who comes into my office notices it. Set in a large, handcrafted 4-foot-by-4-foot frame Luke created for it, the painting shows a wounded man being cared for by a nurse on an anonymous battlefield in the indeterminate past.

One day my friend Barry Taylor came into my office and stood taking in the piece for few minutes while I finished a phone call. When I hung up, Barry said, "Wow! This is a great painting! It reminds me so much of an Odd Nerdrum work." At the time, I only knew of Odd Nerdrum through Luke. I had no idea other people would know his name or recognize his influence in someone else's work. I asked Barry how he could make that correlation. He said he could see the inspiration of Odd in the style and brushstrokes, in the way a person who understands art can do. He said there was a style to the characters and a certain feel that came through. He could sense these subtle connections to the work of this master painter.

Here is the thing: Luke didn't set out to copy Odd in his painting style. He is not making Nerdrum replicas. Instead, he is painting as Luke "in the way of Odd," as it were. When Barry saw the echoes of Odd in Luke's work, it certainly didn't diminish Odd's work or his legacy. Luke isn't trying to make people forget about Odd and pay attention only to Luke. Luke is seeking to be the best painter he can be, and he is inspired by and called forward to do so by Odd's work.

As the student, Luke is on a path to surpass his teacher while painting in his own way. As peculiar as the idea might be, Luke is the greater "Lukan" painter in the way of Odd. Luke is painting from his life, eye, heart, and passion, which have in many ways been influenced by Odd but also remain specifically Luke's. He is not called to be better than Odd; Luke is called to be "greater than" Odd by taking the way of Odd to places that only Luke can go.

Famously, Odd made a point similar to this when describing his experience seeing a Rembrandt for the first time. The way *Wikipedia* tells the story, "Nerdrum had seen Rembrandt's painting, *The Conspiracy of Claudius Civilis* in the National Museum of Fine Arts in Stockholm. Nerdrum says seeing the painting was 'a shock. . . . Pervasive. Like finding home. I can say I found a home in this picture. . . . The wonderful thing with Rembrandt is the confidence he inspires—like when you warm your hands on a stove. Without Rembrandt I would have been so poor.'"[1]

This is one picture of what outdoing Jesus is all about: we take the life of God in us and find its through-line from the life of Jesus to our places of work, our streets, our families, our hearts, our culture.

This is the greater work that we do. Compared to the limited scope of what Jesus did, our work is greater in impact, greater in benefit, and greater in meaning. Which only makes sense. Jesus intended his miraculous signs to have greater implications than the benefit of one person in one place. There is almost no ongoing benefit to the miracles Jesus performed, the food he made available, the suffering he alleviated, the isolation he bridged if the same does not happen in more and greater ways today and every day. All the stories of Jesus would be just stories if we are not doing and outdoing them now.

Moving beyond the Superhero

We like our heroes. And we like to keep our heroes, heroes. We build shrines to them, and we honor them for their particular talents. In sports we have halls of fame. In art we have specialized museums. In music we give awards. Those who make incredible academic, cultural, and scientific advances are awarded internationally recognized prizes. In religion we have the category "saint."

We don't like when our heroes are outdone. It's a bittersweet experience to see a hero's record broken or his or her career fade. We don't like our heroes to be ordinary or fallible. We want there to be special people in the world. Maybe we take comfort in believing that some people aren't affected the way the rest of us are. Whether it's the concept of the superman in the early twentieth century or the gods of Olympus in ancient Greece, we long for someone to rise above the rest of us.

For many of us, the first notion we get that people have special abilities is attached to our parents. I remember sitting in the front seat of our station wagon when I was about six years old and asking my dad, "How do you know where we're going all the time?" As a young boy, I had no real concept of the world outside my block. I could ride my bike with my older sister to the park, and I knew to take a left at the big rock that marked the three-way intersection, but that was pretty much the extent of my navigational skills. But my dad could drive for what seemed like hours and always know where he was, and he could even drive on highways and make all the correct turns to get us to the Dairy Queen. These seemed like superhero abilities to my mind.

As we grow through childhood and into adolescence, many of us flip that scenario of parental hero worship. Leaving behind our childhood versions, we seem to make this shift, and suddenly all we can see is how utterly unprepared our parents seem to be. Their human frailty and weakness are in stark relief to the power they seemed to have had when we were young.

As we reach adulthood, maturity allows us the privilege of freeing our fathers and mothers from the bondage of our childhood idolization and the disillusionment of our adolescence. We begin to learn from them and see them as imperfect masters who walked the path of adulthood before we did.

This is much the same process many of us go through in our understanding of Jesus. We need to free our imaginations of the childhood superhero expectations and move into a deeper understanding of Jesus as our master teacher who calls us to a path of life and faith.

I think Bruce Springsteen, of all people, taps into this sentiment when he writes about Jesus in his autobiography, *Born to Run.*

> As funny as it sounds, I have a "personal" relationship with Jesus. He remains one of my fathers, though as with my own father, I no longer believe in his godly power. I believe deeply in his love, his ability to save . . . but not to damn . . . enough of that. The way I see it, we ate the apple and Adam, Eve, the rebel Jesus in all his glory, and Satan are all part of God's plan to make men and women out of us, to give us the precious gifts of earth, dirt, sweat, blood, sex, sin, goodness, freedom, captivity, love, fear, life and death . . . our humanity and a world of our own.[2]

There is no doubt that the Gospels and the community of Christian faith that has carried on for more than two millennia proclaimed that there is something special about Jesus. Our faith is grounded in the nature of this specialness. Is it something unmatchable by the rest of us? Or was Jesus showing us what humanity can be?

ONE OF THESE IS
NOT LIKE THE OTHERS

The Special Invitation of the Gospel of John

3

The Gospel of John has always presented Bible scholars with some mysteries. It tells stories the other gospels don't tell. It's structured differently, uses language differently, maintains its own order of events, and includes a specific set of miraculous signs that are unique in content and meaning. This gospel is a world unto itself.

There are all kinds of cultural and historical reasons John's Gospel differs from the others, but I believe it is also explicitly crafted to make a special proclamation and invitation: the "they will do greater things" invitation is at the heart of its special nature.

The intentional uniqueness of John's Gospel isn't a cryptic clue evident only to Bible aficionados and scholars. It's revealed right in the text. The gospel makes a special point of saying that it was crafted for a particular outcome. The second to last chapter of the gospel closes with something like a thesis statement: "Then Jesus did many other miraculous signs in his disciples' presence, signs that aren't recorded in this scroll. But these things are written so that you will believe that Jesus is the Christ, God's Son, and that believing, you will have life in his name" (John 20:30–31).

The author of John's Gospel offers a curated set of specific signs recorded in a particular order to produce a deliberate outcome. It's not a neutral account or a biography meant to offer some highlights of Jesus's life. The Gospel of John is a recruitment piece, calling people to follow the selected signs down a particular path.

There's plenty of scholarship on why John tells some stories and not others, so I'm not going to unpack all of that here. Instead, I want to dive into the words used to tell those stories.

To me, the deliberate use of language in this gospel is compelling, particularly the way the author uses the words "believe" and "life." The term "believe" is used more than eighty times in the gospel. You can hardly turn a page without running across the word. It's important to this discussion to clarify terms, specifically the difference between "belief" and "believe." "Belief," as you know, is a noun, and if you are like me, you can hear your elementary school teacher (or *Schoolhouse Rock!*) reminding you, "A noun is a person, place, or thing." Belief functions as a thing, something you can hold or hold to. It's like faith, which is also a noun. "Believe," on the other hand, is obviously a verb. We do believing, and we hold beliefs. This distinction has a significant impact on how we understand the use of the word "believe" in the Gospel of John.

This verb/noun distinction is also true in Greek, the language in which the gospel was written. In Greek, the word for "believe" is *pisteuō*. The noun, "belief," is *pistis*. Just as in English, *pistis* is often used to mean faith.

The Synoptic Gospels of Matthew, Mark, and Luke use both the noun, *pistis*, and the verb, *pisteuō*, repeatedly. The Gospel of John, however, only uses the verb, *pisteuō*. John never uses the noun, *pistis* (belief), not even once!

The lack of use of *pistis* is very unusual. Of the twenty-seven books of the New Testament, twenty-four use the word *pistis*. The three exceptions? The Gospel of John, 2 John, and 3 John. Clearly, this is an intentional choice by the author. I believe it's because the story he's telling calls the audience to the action of believing, not the state of belief.

That has a significant effect on how we understand Jesus saying, "*I assure you that whoever believes in me . . .*" If we interpret the verb "believes" as the noun "belief," we might be led to assume that this assurance is limited to those who hold the proper belief. But when we correctly understand it as a verb, this invitation is for anyone in the act of believing—living in the way of Jesus.

As we explore the miracles in John, we'll see over and over again how Jesus calls people to believe, not to belief. This believing is about doing and outdoing. It's about walking on that same path and living with the same power of God in us, the same power that's in Jesus. Those who believe in Jesus's name do the things Jesus does.

We can see the power in the gospel's intention that "believing, you will have life in his name."

The act of believing, of living in the Jesus way, brings about life.

The Gospel of John also uses the word *zoē*—the term for "life"—a lot, more than forty times, including in the opening poem in chapter 1, "What came into being through the Word was life," and the closing line of chapter 20, "You will have life in his name." By comparison, Matthew uses *zoē* seven times, Luke five times, and Mark only four times. *Zoē* is used 135 times in the

New Testament, and the Gospel of John accounts for nearly one third of those uses. Life is what the Gospel of John is all about.

Another unique feature of this gospel is its frequent pairing of the term "eternal" with life. Just as "believe" is commonly misread as "belief," so is "eternal life" often misunderstood as a reference to the afterlife or heaven. But that's not what "eternal" means. "Eternal" is not referencing a place; it is describing a kind of life. The Gospel of John uses *aiōnios*, which means "without beginning or end, that which always has been and always will be."[1] Jesus does not promise an afterlife with this phrase. He is describing the indelible, abundant, everlasting quality of life.

Jesus is beckoning humanity to a life that has been and always will be—the ancient and present way of life. This gospel is at its core a recruitment piece, beckoning people to an everlasting path of life.

Another unique quality of the Gospel of John is that it serves as a kind of creation story for life on this everlasting path. Creation narratives give people a context for who they are, how they got here, and what they ought to do. All cultures have creation stories. Some have the classic myth-structure, and others are hidden inside history lessons. We mark the creation of our nations with holidays. We have creation stories for our companies on the About Us pages of our websites. We keep alive the creation stories of our relationships by marking anniversaries, telling stories of how we fell in love, and keeping photo albums of how we became a family. We mark our own beginning by celebrating birthdays. There is considerable power in our origin stories, as they help us tell of how and why we were formed and what we hold dear.

The Gospel of John is structured to invoke the power of the Hebrew creation story from the book of Genesis.

> In the beginning was the Word
>> and the Word was with God
>> and the Word was God.
>
> The Word was with God in the beginning.
> Everything came into being through the Word,
>> and without the Word
>> nothing came into being.
>
> What came into being
>> through the Word was life,
>> and the life was the light for all people.
>
> The light shines in the darkness,
>> and the darkness doesn't extinguish the light.
>
> (John 1:1–5)

Consider a few of the many structural elements of John that connect to the Genesis narrative:

- Both begin with poems as their prologue. The power, beauty, and truthfulness of poetry have been part of the faith of the Hebrew people and Christians from their very beginnings. In the beginning, there was a poem.
- "In the beginning" actually starts both poems.
- There are seven miraculous signs in John, and seven days in the creation narrative of Genesis.

- The Word is connected to creation: in Genesis, "God said, and it was," and in John, "In the beginning was the Word. . . . Everything came into being through the Word."
- Both use *light* with *life*. "And there was darkness on all the land, and God said let there be light, and there was light." In John's version, the light was for all people, "What came into being through the Word was life, and the life was the light for all people."

The poem continues:

Those who did welcome him,
    those who believed in his name,
    he authorized to become God's children,
    born not from blood
    nor from human desire or passion,
    but born from God.
The Word became flesh
    and made his home among us.
We have seen his glory,
    glory like that of a father's only son,
    full of grace and truth.

(John 1:12–14)

John's story is about how a people living in light came about. The similarities continue in the way each account frames the story of a people and their heritage. The Genesis account starts in a garden and centers around Adam. The family line that follows includes Adam and Eve and runs through Sarah and Abraham, Isaac and Rebekah, Joseph, and all the way to Moses. It is a story of a people—who they were, where they came from, and who came from them. Patriarchal lineage was important to the Hebrew people; it gave heft to someone's story by connecting that person to the family line. In the Gospel of Luke, for example, Jesus's lineage is traced back through Jewish history to inform Luke's readers that Jesus is the promised Messiah. The climax of this list is "Jared son of Mahalalel son of Cainan son of Enos son of Seth son of Adam son of God" (Luke 3:38).

The Gospel of John's creation story is not based on lineage and patriarchal lines. In fact, no names are mentioned at all. Instead, it makes the point that people are in the family of God regardless of their bloodline. They are born of God. The Gospel of John replaces the narratives of familial tribes with an invitation into the family of God. Anyone who was active in the way of Jesus, who *believed in his name*, was part of this family. This story removes restrictions so that all people see themselves as members of the full family of God. When Jesus encounters those outside the chosen lineage, he calls them brothers and sisters in the family of God. Later in the gospel, we see that what was true of Jesus is true for everyone in the family—we are children of the same source.

Jesus as the Son of God[2] is not the exception but the brother in a new humanity. This story explores what this humanity looks like, lives like, loves like. This is a creation story of a new way of being.

The key to this vision of humanity is found in the seven miraculous signs we'll be exploring. Even this terminology is important. The Gospel of John does not refer to these stories as "miracles" but as "miraculous signs." As you may have already guessed, "miraculous signs" is a phrase used only in the Gospel of John.

Again, this is intentional. The author of the gospel is making it clear that these miracles are indicators of something; they are signs that point us to something more grand, more wonderful, more important, more repeatable than the details of the miracles. These seven select stories show us a tangible vision for a participatory way of life.

In the remainder of the book we will explore these seven miraculous signs, seeing how they show us the path for creating a celebratory, empathic, empowered, abundant, fearless, participatory, fully engaged here-and-now way of living for all of humanity. We will see how people are living this reality now all around the world and how these miraculous signs were intended to call all of us to greater works from the very start.

CELEBRATION

That Time the Wine Ran Out

On the third day there was a wedding in Cana of Galilee. Jesus' mother was there, and Jesus and his disciples were also invited to the celebration. When the wine ran out, Jesus' mother said to him, "They don't have any wine."

Jesus replied, "Woman, what does that have to do with me? My time hasn't come yet."

His mother told the servants, "Do whatever he tells you." Nearby were six stone water jars used for the Jewish cleansing ritual, each able to hold about twenty or thirty gallons.

Jesus said to the servants, "Fill the jars with water," and they filled them to the brim. Then he told them, "Now draw some from them and take it to the headwaiter," and they did. The headwaiter tasted the water that had become wine. He didn't know where it came from, though the servants who had drawn the water knew.

The headwaiter called the groom and said, "Everyone serves the good wine first. They bring out the second-rate wine only when the guests are drinking freely. You kept the good wine until now." This was the first miraculous sign that Jesus did in Cana of Galilee.

John 2:1–11

As the first in the set of seven miraculous signs in John, this one seems an odd pick. At the risk of sounding sacrilegious, it's really not all that impressive. At least as miracles go.

If the Gospels were trying to show how otherworldly Jesus was by his miraculous acts, they might tell about how Jesus could—I don't know—*fly*. I mean, *really* showcase Jesus as a miracle worker not bound by the laws of nature. Instead, the author starts the entire set with something that has all the punch of a party trick. A pastor friend of mine, Josh Scott, put it this way: "When I preached on this passage at our church, I was struck by how it feels like an ideal miracle for college students. Why would the writer choose this as the first miraculous sign in his record of the life of Jesus?"

Here's what I think: The miraculous signs are not about Jesus breaking the laws of physics; they are about Jesus breaking open human potential. These signs are not intended as power displays. Something far more invitational and inclusive is going on with these stories.

Maybe you noticed that Jesus performed this miraculous sign reluctantly after some prodding by his mother. It was done in a way that kept the attention of the crowd away from Jesus and on the groom. Those who knew that a miraculous sign had taken place—Jesus, his disciples, his mother, and the servants—didn't announce the miracle to the wedding guests. Jesus wasn't trying to draw attention to his power. The outcome of the miracle was that people had more to drink; the celebration, and the reputation of the groom, was saved.

Pour a Drink

What is helpful to know about the first century is that suitable drink was tough to come by. At its core, this story is about changing undrinkable water into something drinkable. And that was done by making wine. We tend to see wine as a luxury drink, but in the first century wine represented something to drink that was not contaminated. To the first-century mind, this water-into-wine sign pointed to a critical issue that went well beyond one wedding party. It touched on survival itself.

While we tend to think the problem of undrinkable water is solved by removing pollutants and making water purer, for the bulk of human history, drinkable liquid came through boiling, fermenting, or distilling. The development of wine was crucial in providing a drinking source to much of the Mesopotamian world. Wine and other alcohol were a primary source of drink all the way into the eighteenth century.

In his book *A History of the World in 6 Glasses*, author Tom Standage tells how civilization advanced from the Stone Age to the twenty-first century through the development of beer, wine, spirits, coffee, tea, and cola. Standage shows how the development of wine and beer opened up travel by offering journeyers a long-lasting, portable drink. Even the productivity gains in mid-seventeenth-century England can be traced to the creation of coffeehouses, which provided the public something safe to drink.

What Jesus does in this story is being done today in incredible ways all around the world. People are performing amazing feats of alchemy by changing undrinkable liquid into life-saving water. As impressive as it was to turn water into wine, to see human sewage being transformed into pure drinking water for millions is a greater-than extension of this miracle.

The people at Janicki Bioenergy have created a wastewater treatment method that converts human sewage and waste into clean, drinkable water in a matter of minutes. The Omniprocessor produces water from the waste, then incinerates the remaining waste solids to create an energy source.

This machine produces clean, drinkable water for forty-three thousand people from the waste of one hundred thousand people each day. This incredible cycle from human waste to drinkable water to an energy source is the kind of greater-than work imperative for human health and flourishing today.

This purification process, along with astounding leaps in desalinization that allow seawater to be turned into drinkable water and the ability to convert dew collected at night in the desert into a reliable water source, is helping people across the African continent who have suffered devastating consequences from a shortage of water. Turning the undrinkable into the drinkable results in widespread cultural transformation that especially benefits women and girls who typically spend days collecting water from polluted rivers and then boiling it. Access to clean water allows them time to explore school, business, and creativity.

Providing usable water has an enormous impact on reducing the war and conflict that sit at the heart of so much poverty and human suffering. More than two billion people across the world do not have access to clean water or proper sanitation; this results in the deaths of over seven hundred thousand children each year. There are real fears that if water is not made available to the growing populations around the world, conflicts over water will lead to war.

Saving Celebration and Saving Honor

The water-to-wine story is set inside the story of a wedding celebration. Jesus is called by his mother to save the celebration, for the party had run out of wine. Many people have a hard time seeing Jesus in the role of making sure people have enough alcohol to drink at a wedding party. It strikes them as odd that Jesus would be into saving parties by providing alcohol. It feels less like the opening miracle of a gospel and more like the scene from *Talladega Nights* where the characters are discussing how they should pray before a meal. Their ridiculous conversation turns to how they think about Jesus. The character Cal Naughton Jr. says, "I like to picture Jesus in a tuxedo T-shirt, because it says, like, I want to be formal, but I'm here to party too. 'Cuz I like to party, so I like my Jesus to party." Some people have trouble wrapping their heads around the idea of Jesus as the party savior.

People need celebration, relaxation, and recreation to be healthy human beings. The structure of the Hebrew faith is built around the Sabbath, a day of rest and celebration on a weekly basis. Stan Mitchell, a Christian pastor and scholar who knows an unusual amount of detail about Jewish weddings of the first century, helped me understand this story when he mentioned that ancient weddings were multiple-day affairs. He noted the significance in the opening line of the story: "On the third day there was a wedding in Cana of Galilee." That was the day the vows took place. The two previous days were celebration days, when the families met to practice their new "one family" customs. The third day was when the couple "became one," so it was important that this day be a success.

In the gospel account, something had gone wrong. The hosts were about to run out of wine on the most important day. Apparently, because of customary hospitality expectations, this would have carried great shame for the groom. Turning the water into wine is not used to enhance Jesus's reputation at the party; it's used to save the reputation of the groom. The groom allows Jesus's mother, Jesus, and the servants to join with him in making the celebration a success. The story makes a point of having Jesus's mother notice that they are going to run out of wine. She is the one who saw the social impact. She is the one who brought together the resources needed for the bride and groom to be supported and the guests to continue their important cultural engagement.

Nasir Sobhani does something similar by being the "the streets barber." His story is chronicled in a fantastic and heart-stirring video. On his one day off each week, Nasir takes to the streets to give haircuts to homeless people. This intimate act of connection not only transforms the person's appearance but also seems to change the person's entire affect.

In the video, Nasir talks with a man about his struggles. The man says, "I drink because I like alcohol." Nasir says to him, candidly and straightforwardly, "Think about it. You drink because you feel lonely." The man's face softens as if he has been understood for the first time in a long time. He agrees and says, "Yeah, I drink because I feel lonely." Nasir reaches out and puts his hand on the man's shoulder.

Nasir has taken time to support this man, to help him care for his hair and beard, to celebrate the man and his life. He is not there to lay blame or take credit. He's there to share his gift, and that gift helped the man see himself free of the shame—at least for a while—that so often goes with being unemployed or homeless.

Arron Westondorp is part of my church in Minneapolis and lives with Moebius syndrome, a craniofacial/neurological condition. He is not able to speak, so he types on an iPad on his wheelchair, and it turns his typing into speech.

When he was nine years old, he was granted a trip to Disney World by the Make-A-Wish Foundation. "I went to Disney World with them twenty-three years ago," he told me, "and it still has an impact on me to this day." Arron said they honored him by taking his needs seriously and making it possible for him to stay in a hotel, ride in a van, fly on an airplane, and visit "the most magical place on earth." For a nine-year-old, this was an ultimate celebration.

Celebration, freedom from shame, the recognition of shared humanity—these are the undercurrents of Jesus's miraculous sign. Today, some do this vital work as a profession while others engage in it less formally. They are the persons in their families, friendships, and work environments who make sure people are recognized, cheered on, and celebrated. They remember birthdays and anniversaries. They are quick to celebrate the accomplishments of others. They are committed to finding ways to change a bedroom into a place of celebration or to imbue an otherwise sterile workroom with a party atmosphere. They "turn water into wine" in different ways.

Purification to Celebration

The water-to-wine story is more significant than merely changing the chemical makeup of water. It includes changing that which has been set aside as holy. In fact, the story goes to great lengths to indicate that the water was from jars that were used for religious purification.

The jars seem to be an essential detail. Indeed, we know more about the jars than about most anything else in the story: We don't know whose wedding it is. We don't know why Jesus's mother is concerned with the amount of wine. We don't know why Jesus is there. But we are made aware that there were six jars, that they were made of stone, that they could hold between twenty and thirty gallons each, and that the water in them was used for ritual purification. Something about those jars must be important.

The ritual cleansing practices of first-century Jewish communities not only produced sanitary benefits but also made people acceptable for inclusion in religious activities. So, when this story has Jesus change water that was meant for religious purification into wine, it is making a not-so-subtle statement about how that which has been set aside for religious purposes could be used for the benefit of people. This has great resonance with Jesus's teaching about how even the Sabbath, the most holy of days, was created for the benefit of humanity and not the other way around. This element of Jesus turning the understood religious narrative on its head happens in all seven of the miraculous signs.

These signs point not only to what we are capable of in the physical sense but also to how we can be free of any narrative, religious or not, that considers something more valuable than people. This is among the more important implications of these miraculous signs of Jesus, and they are about expanding what people believe is possible. They are agents of change not only in the physical elements but also in the hearts, minds, and imaginations of people who hear about the signs. In this way, they are not only signs that point back but also signs that point to what could be. This is what we begin to see in the story line of the Gospel of John, as the word starts to spread about what is possible.

EMPATHY

That Time Things Broke Good

5

He returned to Cana in Galilee where he had turned the water into wine. In Capernaum there was a certain royal official whose son was sick. When he heard that Jesus was coming from Judea to Galilee, he went out to meet him and asked Jesus if he would come and heal his son, for his son was about to die. Jesus said to him, "Unless you see miraculous signs and wonders, you won't believe."

The royal official said to him, "Lord, come before my son dies."

Jesus replied, "Go home. Your son lives." The man believed the word that Jesus spoke to him and set out for his home.

While he was on his way, his servants were already coming to meet him. They said, "Your son lives!" So he asked them at what time his son had started to get better. And they said, "The fever left him yesterday at about one o'clock in the afternoon." Then the father realized that this was the hour when Jesus had said to him, "Your son lives." And he and his entire household believed in Jesus. This was the second miraculous sign Jesus did while going from Judea to Galilee.

John 4:46–54

Perhaps, like me, you are struck by the strangeness of the end of the passage. It seems a bit odd that in a story so filled with action, the narrator wants to bring the reader back to the miraculous sign count. It might be odd, or it might be a genius way for the storyteller to remind us that there is something important about the selection of the stories and the number of them.

When we consider that the author selected the stories he used in the Gospel of John with a specific agenda in mind, we can see how this rather strange-sounding aside serves as a clue to the intentionality of the story selection. The phrase "miraculous sign" is one of the clues that has alerted scholars and careful readers to the use of a numerical device to connect this gospel to the Genesis creation story with its seven-days structure.

Also, this story is one of only three miraculous signs of the healing variety in the gospel. Some are surprised that John contains only three healing stories. Many people assume that the majority of the miracles of Jesus are healings. And while that may be true in the Gospels of Matthew, Mark, and Luke, in John healings make up not quite half of the miraculous signs.

That is not to take anything away from the importance of the healings or the significance of this particular sign. But when there is a healing in the Gospel of John, it's a doozy. And that is indeed the case with this one.

There is an almost understated feel to this story. At first reading, all the layers of significance could be easily missed. This is a story in which a tremendous amount of meaning is conveyed in very simple phrases. While the story centers around the healing of a young boy with a fever, this story contains multiple "breakings": breaking fevers, breaking social boundaries, and breaking expectations.

All three of these "breakings" are meaningful for us as we consider the implications for the new way of humanity.

Breaking Fevers

While breaking the young boy's fever is the first dilemma, the story gives no details about that fever other than its life-threatening nature. The lack of specificity allows this story to connect with the universal experience of sick children from around the world. While children dying of fevers is incredibly rare in the United States where I live, and is decreasing numerically around the world, it remains the leading cause of death for children around the globe. Fevers are wickedly dangerous to children, so it's clear why this boy's father was willing to go to anyone who might help, make any sacrifice, take on any new belief to save his child.

This is the emotional setting of our story. We are drawn by the desperation of a father seeking hope. He is chasing the rumors he heard of a wandering healer from the town of Cana, a day's walk away. Maybe word got out about the wine incident from the wedding there, or perhaps he heard other stories. Cana makes sense as the place where he would go because it seems to be Jesus's hometown—it's mentioned more than any place other than Jerusalem in the Gospel of John. Jesus's family is there; he goes to weddings there; some of his disciples are from there. People would know to find him in Cana.

The interaction between Jesus and the father is a short one. Jesus speaks only fifteen words in this entire engagement. Five of them are "Go home. Your son lives," and even odder is the ten-word statement "Unless you see miraculous signs and wonders, you won't believe." Jesus says this just after the father asked Jesus to accompany him to his town to heal his son. It seems like an odd thing to say to a desperate man who has just asked you to use your power to save his son's life.

We meet Jesus speaking to all those around him so they will know that they need to pay attention to these signs to understand what Jesus's agenda is all about. The message Jesus shares with those around him is "unless you are able to see this larger story of the way of humanity and God through this miraculous sign, you will not believe, and then you will not find life in this way." Jesus is changing hearts and minds about God, humanity, and the story of life; he's not just solving individual problems of wine shortages, illnesses, blindness, or any of the particular contexts of the miracles.

The healing of the fever is almost a passing event in the story. Jesus simply declares that the father's son lives. Then a day later the father learns that the declaration was a true one.

Among the teachings in this story is that of ongoing belief in the absence of knowing.

As impressive as the healing miracles in this gospel are, they are limited in their overall benefit and their scope. In this story, one boy is saved from dying from a fever. That death-preventing action is quite short lived. The boy will presumably die later in life. The boy is not transformed into some sort of superhuman mutant who is immune from all fevers and is never vulnerable to illness again. Yet this does not take away from the meaningfulness of this story, even as it shows how limited it is. What is more impressive than the onetime healing of one boy is the work of those who have sought to change the circumstances in which children are sick with fevers that lead to death. In each miracle, we meet Jesus calling us to do even greater works—in this one everything from saving one boy from a fever to changing health conditions so that kids don't get fevers in the first place.

Saving children's lives is not only right for the children and their families but also critical for the survival of humanity. In the last two hundred years, the rate at which children have died worldwide has decreased significantly. In 1800, 43 percent of the world's newborns died before their fifth birthday. In 1960, child mortality for those under five was still 18.5 percent. In 2015, it was down to 4.3 percent.[1]

The development of vaccines has changed the narrative from working to break fevers to preventing them all around the world. In my lifetime alone we have seen the eradication or near eradication of the kinds of diseases that have killed millions of children, including smallpox, whooping cough, measles, tuberculosis, rinderpest, polio, Guinea worm disease, tetanus, malaria, and the deadly Hib disease.

Modern medicine has played a significant role in the reduction of child mortality, and we should be proud of these incredible medical accomplishments. But more substantial reasons for the global reduction in child mortality rates from nearly half of children dying before age five to fewer than one in twenty are changes in infrastructure, specifically sanitation.

New approaches in urban planning, water supplies, and farmers' growing patterns, as well as the work being done by civil engineers, nutritionists, and sanitation workers, have brought us the greatest amount of healing the world has ever seen. The global ability to provide food that is not contaminated and water that is fit to drink, and to dispose properly of human waste, has changed entire countries and human civilization.

It is easy to think that people who work the back of a sanitation truck or dig a water well or maintain sewer systems are doing menial work that is anything but miraculous. But modern-day miracle workers are not only keeping children from dying of fevers, they are also keeping them from getting sick in the first place.

One of those modern-day miracle workers is the Karibu Loo company in Nairobi. Karibu means "welcome" in Swahili, and "loo" is the English word for bathroom, which is well understood due to Nairobi's colonial British past. The company's name means "Welcome Toilet." Perfect.

Karibu Loo provides what we in the United States would call portable bathrooms. Those little hard-plastic structures that often feel like a total last resort to many of us. In many parts of the world they are a tremendous upgrade not only for the dignity of privacy they provide but also for their sanitation and health benefits. Its bright red color well identifies the Karibu Loo brand. These standout "loos" have made an incredible difference in Nairobi.

Many places in Nairobi don't have permanent toilets, such as where football matches take place or where villages hold their celebrations, weddings, and school meetings. Where there are people, there is the need for a loo. So these bright red plastic huts are keeping water clean, hands clean, and stomachs free of infections. This is the result of having safe, consistent, and clean portable sanitation.

I met one of the founders of Karibu Loo at a fun run conducted by the Portable Sanitation Association International (PSAI). (The fact that there is an international association for those who provide portable sanitation tells you how important this service is globally.) The PSAI was holding its annual conference in conjunction with World Toilet Day on November 19. Yes, you read that right.

Let me tell you, these people take the power of the toilet seriously. And they should. The toilet has literally been a lifesaver for millions of people. The World Toilet Day website has a quote from the deputy secretary-general of the United Nations: "We have the tools, let's make it happen." The "it" there is the worldwide goal of everyone having access to a household toilet by 2030. People around the world are working hard to bring sanitation to everyone on the planet. That is a "greater things" kind of goal.

If you are looking for some inspiration today, go to www .WorldToiletDay.info. There you will find inspiring stories, mind-bending details on the flow of "poo" across the planet, and more details than you can imagine about human waste, including including a link to The WHO/UNICEF Joint Monitoring Programme for Water Supply, Sanitation and Hygiene Report of the Progress on Drinking Water, Sanitation and Hygiene.

These people know their "business." Oh, and they don't miss a chance at a potty pun. But don't be fooled by their good-natured attitude; they are sanitation serious. Inspired by the health benefits of sanitation, the people at Karibu Loo have expanded their business opportunities to help fund the education of the most impoverished kids in Nairobi. All profits from their sanitation business go to fund education and support children in the slum of Dagoretti whose lives are affected by HIV/AIDS.

Breaking Social Boundaries

A cursory reading of the story of the young boy with fever might make you think it's a story where Jesus is the hero and the young boy is the beneficiary, and there is good reason to think that. But the father of the young boy gives us a fresh understanding of why this story is included in the gospel and what it points to: before the breaking of a fever, another kind of breaking was needed—the breaking of social barriers designed to keep someone like the father of the boy away from someone like Jesus. It might be easy to miss the importance of a man who was part of the Roman military system traveling to another village and seeking out a Jewish mystic and asking him for a favor. This kind of engagement meant breaking all sorts of cultural and ethnic barriers.

We see from the way the story is told how significant this interaction was from the very start.

The story setting was dramatic. When a Roman soldier approached a Jewish man, any encounter between the two was by definition riddled with tension, power dynamics, and danger. While this is a short story, there is significant meaning packed into "In Capernaum there was a certain royal official whose son was sick. When he heard that Jesus was coming from Judea to Galilee, he went out to meet him and asked Jesus if he would come and heal his son, for his son was about to die."

The term "royal official" conveyed that this man was not a Jew but a gentile, and that he had power. The Jewish people were under occupation by the Romans. We still see similar settings in many places around the world where distinctions are made between people. The distinction of Jews from gentiles was not the kind of discrimination people had a choice about or were making out of their own bigotry or personal fear. The separation was rooted in the identity of both groups and could be traced to the time when the Israelites were in exile in Babylon. Being a people of their own and not melting into the culture of the Babylonians were required for the Israelites' survival. And survival is among the most powerful motives for tribal distinction. That is the thing about tribal, ethnic, religious separation: people rarely engage in it as a matter of personal choice. This isn't unique to the Jews and gentiles of the first century. It is a part of the human experience. To be human is to be tribal. It is our biases and prejudices and tribal assumptions that Jesus calls us to set aside for something greater.

Credit should be given to this gentile father; he was the first to make a move over the boundary. Perhaps it was the power of a father's love for his son. The official traveled more than a day to Cana to find a man of whom he had heard a rumor of his miraculous doings.

The father was at the end of his rope. In the text we meet a man with no other options: "If you don't come now, my son will die." You can feel the burden, the pain that it takes for a father to leave his son. And the desperation involved in going to a man from another, "lesser," culture to ask for his help.

Overcoming the culturally assumed "distance" between the men put them both at risk. There was significant risk for the father to go for help from what he must have thought was a wandering Jewish mystic of whom he had heard only rumors. And this was risky for Jesus and his followers as well. For he was not only helping a gentile but also giving aid to the enemy in the system. He was bringing life to a boy who would grow up to be part of the enemy force.

What we see in both men is an act of empathy. Jesus was drawn by the father into his situation. The father was drawn into Jesus's land because he needed what Jesus offered. These two were affecting each other. This is not a story of Jesus wanting to step over the gentile boundary but a story of the humanity of another pulling Jesus over that boundary. Willingly, I might add. Still, Jesus seems to be at the mercy of the reality he is living in. This is what connection with another person creates: a pull over the line. In this story, you can see the truth of the idea that you cannot be human while violating the humanity of another.

Perhaps you know the story of Mohammad Gulab and Marcus Luttrell. It too is a story of two men connecting with each other's shared humanity over cultural boundaries. Luttrell was part of a United States Special Forces team in Afghanistan. On June 27, 2005, his unit came under attack, and he was separated from his unit and significantly injured. After a number of days, he was discovered by Mohammad Gulab.

Mohammad was part of the Pashtun clan that lived in the area. He took Marcus into his home, fed him, kept him safe, and helped him heal under the teaching of Pashtunwali, an unwritten ethical code that governs the Pashtun people and means "the way of the Pashtuns" or "the code of life." Mohammad Gulab understood that obligation to mean that he was to care for Marcus Luttrell as his most-honored guest.

Rumors spread around the village that an American soldier had been wounded and was being kept safe. One of the commanders of the Afghan insurgency, Qari Moued Safi, made a public call for Marcus to be turned over to him by saying, "Pashtunwali does not extend to helping oppressors and infidel aggressors such as that American soldier who is an enemy of Islam."[2]

Mohammad Gulab and his entire family were at risk of retaliation for aiding the enemy. But Mohammad said, "We did not rescue Marcus for money or privileges. By rescuing and keeping him safe for five nights in our home, we were only doing our cultural obligation."

This "cultural obligation" is another way of saying "a way of life." At its core, it's about caring for and protecting another human life, even if that is the life of one's declared enemy. This is what matches the life and teaching of Jesus. This is what we see in this story of a father of a sick son and Jesus: that it is possible to see the difference and for that difference to be a means of connection rather than separation. In many ways, we see in the Mohammad Gulab and Marcus Luttrell story a kind of rhyming with the story of the father of the sick boy and Jesus.

In this story of the father of a sick boy we see a vision of the new humanity, as the father walked into the unknown places to seek out the "other" whom he believed could have a gift for his son. It was the father who first saw God in the "other." This man was convinced that he could be part of what God was doing in the life of Jesus and held out the hope that could change his son. That is a kind of faith of the new humanity: to see in the "other" that which we need. Perhaps this is what prompted Jesus to say, "Your faith has already healed your son."

Breaking Expectations (God Boxes)

There is a third breaking in the story: a breaking of expectations, setting God free from the confines of Jesus. There is an exciting interaction in this story. The father wants Jesus to go with him to his house and heal his son. But Jesus doesn't go. Instead, he declares the boy's healing from a distance—"Go home. Your son lives."

The man believes him and heads for home. But on the way he meets servants from his house, and they confirm that the fever broke at the time he was talking with Jesus. This realization is the turning point for the entire family.

When Jesus says, "Your son lives," the father believes it. He becomes the first person in the Gospel of John to believe and act upon his belief in an unbound God. It is as if the writer of the story wants us to see in this man a picture of humanity not only removed from its boundaries around one another but also removed from its boundaries around God.

There is this wonderful subtext in the story where the father wanted to bring the miracle worker to the place where his son was for the healing to take place. You can't blame the man for believing that the works of God are bound in space and time. It is common for all of us to believe that there are some places or some people wherein the power of God dwells.

Jesus opens the story of God by essentially saying to the man, "I don't need to accompany you to the place where your son is for the healing of God to be available to him." This story, as much as any we will look at, has a mystical sense of changing the expectations of space and time to it.

In this story, we witness the power of God living in and through Jesus, without being bound to him. God is not limited to the places where Jesus is. This God without boundaries sits right at the heart of the proclamation that "those will do the works that I do and do even greater works than these by the same power that is alive in me."

EMPOWERMENT

That Time at the Pool

6

After this there was a Jewish festival, and Jesus went up to Jerusalem. In Jerusalem near the Sheep Gate in the north city wall is a pool with the Aramaic name Bethsaida. It had five covered porches, and a crowd of people who were sick, blind, lame, and paralyzed sat there. A certain man was there who had been sick for thirty-eight years. When Jesus saw him lying there, knowing that he had already been there a long time, he asked him, "Do you want to get well?"

The sick man answered him, "Sir, I don't have anyone who can put me in the water when it is stirred up. When I'm trying to get to it, someone else has gotten in ahead of me."

Jesus said to him, "Get up! Pick up your mat and walk." Immediately the man was well, and he picked up his mat and walked. Now that day was the Sabbath.

The Jewish leaders said to the man who had been healed, "It's the Sabbath; you aren't allowed to carry your mat."

He answered, "The man who made me well said to me, 'Pick up your mat and walk.'"

They inquired, "Who is this man who said to you, 'Pick it up and walk'?" The man who had been cured didn't know who it was, because Jesus had slipped away from the crowd gathered there.

Later Jesus found him in the temple and said, "See! You have been made well. Don't sin anymore in case something worse happens to you." The man went and proclaimed to the Jewish leaders that Jesus was the man who had made him well.

As a result, the Jewish leaders were harassing Jesus, since he had done these things on the Sabbath. Jesus replied, "My Father is still working, and I am working too." For this reason the Jewish leaders wanted even more to kill him—not only because he was doing away with the Sabbath but also because he called God his own Father, thereby making himself equal with God.

John 5:1–18

I have a confession to make. I've never really liked this story. I'm not entirely sure why, but I have had an apathetic feeling toward it for as long as I can remember, including well into writing this book. Over the past year, while working on this book and telling people I was writing about the seven miraculous signs in the Gospel of John, I'd forget about this one. I had a hard time even remembering the details of the story—for some reason, they didn't matter much to me. I suspect my inability to emotionally connect with it was due to the complexity of the story line. There are a lot of moving parts in this one: a man who can't walk, a mat, a set of pools, a gate, a question, a conversation, a negative response to the healing. I just couldn't find handholds to keep me invested.

Just as I'm not sure what caused my disconnect, I'm not sure what caused that to change. But change it did. I now count this story as my favorite of the seven. Perhaps it was because I spent more time in the story and began to see it as one of the signs pointing humanity on a path of a new way of living, but whatever the reason, I now see the inherent drama in the story's complexity, and I love it. The subtle, powerful meaning of nearly every sentence has embedded the story deeply in my imagination. I find myself referencing this story in conversations with friends, in counseling situations, and in sermons, at what I fear is a level of "overdoing it." I'm captured by this sign's clarion call for human empowerment and its explicit critique of systems, especially religious systems, that are concerned more with their own preservation than with benefiting people and human thriving.

A Word of Caution about Healing Stories

In the miracle stories in the Gospel of John, Jesus never asks about the faith of the people at the center of the story. There are no quid pro quos—a miracle for a statement of faith. Quite to the contrary, those being healed often have no idea what happened or even who healed them.

Consider the three miraculous signs we have looked at to this point and keep this in mind as we look at the next four. In the first miracle, the groom who was the "beneficiary" was not even aware that Jesus was involved in the miracle. In the second, the miracle was performed at a distance, and while the father was aware of Jesus's participation, the son, whose fever broke, was an unknowing beneficiary. In this third miracle, the man at the center of the story didn't know anything about Jesus, not even his name. It was only later when they connected in the temple that he was able to identify Jesus as the person who made him well.

Don't miss the significance of anonymity in these stories. There is no correlation between the miraculous sign and the person having faith. There is no correlation between the sign and belief in or even knowledge of Jesus. There is not a hint of the expectation that the recipients of the benefits of these works are connected to their knowledge of or belief in Jesus in any way. In fact, all seven signs are accomplished without any faith participation of the recipients. To the contrary, most of the time there is considerable confusion about what happened and who did what. In the Gospel of John, there is no "for the believers only" story line.

The Pool by the Sheep Gate

The power and meaning of this sign are found not only in what happened (a man being healed so that he could stand, walk, and carry his mat) but also in the details of who participated, when it happened, and where it took place. While it might not be evident at first reading, the setting reveals the personal heartache and human empowerment that are at the center of this story.

Consider the description: "In Jerusalem near the Sheep Gate in the north city wall is a pool with the Aramaic name Bethsaida. It had five covered porches, and a crowd of people who were sick, blind, lame, and paralyzed sat there." A large pool surrounded by people who suffer from all kinds of maladies paints quite the picture. The reader is drawn into this scene and can imagine the kind of heartache and pain that exists as people, apparently, believed they would be healed if they got into the pool precisely when the waters were stirred.

The story tells us that this place was near the Sheep Gate on the north end of the city wall. This gate was used to bring sheep into the temple to be washed and prepared for sacrifice. This was the animal entrance. This was the place where the sacrifice ritual would begin. We know little about this pool, except that it was near the place where the sheep were washed, so it is clear that this was not some healing spa but perhaps a place for the throwaways of society. At any rate, this is where people who were sick, blind, lame, and paralyzed were sent.

In all the time I was working on this book and talking about this story, I mistakenly referred to it as the "healing of the paralyzed man" story. On some level, it was a reasonable assumption. I thought he was paralyzed because the pool is described as a place where people who were sick, blind, lame, and paralyzed sat. My assumption is supported by Jesus saying to the man, "Pick up your mat and walk." But the story doesn't say the man was paralyzed. It just says he was sick: "A certain man was there who had been sick for thirty-eight years. When Jesus saw him lying there, knowing that he had already been there a long time, he asked him, 'Do you want to get well?'"

There is real power and pain in language that generalizes, miscategorizes, and limits a person. If this were the only time I had ever overgeneralized a person's disabilities, I could set it aside as a Bible-reading problem. But that's not the case. As embarrassing as it is, I must confess that I get uncomfortable being around people with significant physical struggles, and I tend to avoid those situations. That avoidance leads to me not seeing the specifics of people's context and circumstances. The story of the man on the mat is an invitation to reset my (and perhaps your) engagement with assumptions. This is a story about change—about changing a situation, but also about changing a possibility and a power dynamic.

Jesus's interaction with this man pulls us even further from our assumptions when he questions the man's understanding and not his physical limitations. Jesus asks, "Do you want to get well?" How about that for a question? It might strike you as a bit rude or confusing. Perhaps you assume that anyone who has a sickness that has limited his life would want to get well. That's not always the case. This man had lived with this condition for thirty-eight years. To cope with long-term chronic conditions, many people make life adjustments and accommodations that can push the pursuit of healing off the list of priorities. I was talking with a friend who struggles with a chronic illness who has figured out how to live her life with her limitation and found ways to turn it into opportunity. She said her focus is no longer on getting "better" but on living her life to the fullest.

I am in no way suggesting that this man is responsible for his illness. What I am saying is that at some point a man has the right to simply say, "I have chosen my path, and I am not pursuing healing any longer." That can be empowering, but at the same time it engages what therapists refer to as learned helplessness.

Learned helplessness occurs when a person or animal endures repeatedly painful or otherwise aversive stimuli that it is unable to escape or avoid. Research has shown that increased 5-HT (serotonin) activity in the dorsal raphe nucleus plays a critical role in learned helplessness. Other key brain regions involved with the expression of helpless behavior include the basolateral amygdala, central nucleus of the amygdala, and bed nucleus of the stria terminalis. Activity in the medial prefrontal cortex, dorsal hippocampus, septum, and hypothalamus has also been observed during states of helplessness.[1]

Jesus is not coming in with a predetermined agenda. He starts by wanting to know if there is something this man wants, something Jesus can participate in. Empowering another human being with the capacities the person already has is at the heart of the new humanity. This is what makes Jesus's question "Do you want to get better?" such a kind and gracious one. It does not assume that what he would want for the man is what the man wants for himself.

We don't know anything about this man at all from the story. The story does not tell us why Jesus picked the man or whether there was something special about him. These gospel stories are not reserved for people with extraordinary sets of circumstances.

This story is a helpful reminder as we deal with other people and the stories that frame their lives. We know shockingly little about what has brought any person to the place that person is in or about the story of how he or she got there. The stories we tell ourselves about the situations we are in are more important than the particular facts themselves. Even if we think we know a person very well, we know only bits and pieces of the person's experiences. Spouses don't know all there is to know about even their lover of five decades. Parents don't know all there is to know about their children's situation or mind-set. We don't even know everything we could know about ourselves. In one sense, we are all strangers, even to ourselves. This is why the question, "What do *you* want?" is crucial to genuine engagement. Asking another person what he or she wants is key to the kind of full human engagement we are called to on the path Jesus treads.

I am struck that the man in the story never gives an explicit "Yes! I want to be well." The man's response—"I don't have anyone who can put me in the water when it is stirred up"—is heartbreaking. Here is a man who feels he lacks the resources he needs, and he is alone. This is a far too familiar story of someone being isolated and feeling powerless.

Often when I'm looking at the stories of the Gospels, I like to look with others and compare notes, as I did with my friend Kurty. A conversation about this miracle led to a discussion about advancements in prosthetics. No longer just a hunk of plastic intended to support some weight or give the appearance of a limb, prosthetics now help people who have lost limbs use their own neuro-pathways to move an artificial limb. Kurty said, "The real miracle is the first person who said, 'Even though your leg was blown off, we can find a way for you to walk again.'" I totally got what she was saying. Often, it's having the idea of something being possible that takes the biggest leap of faith.

Kurty is a really bright thinker. She is doing graduate study in the hermeneutics of the Gospels—what the setting was, why the authors wrote in the way they did, what the audience in the first century would have heard in these stories, that sort of thing. Kurty said what you see in the story of Jesus is the fulfillment of the ancient Jewish imagination—that God wants fullness and wholeness for all of humanity. "This wholeness is not simply about a foot at the end of a leg. It is the very idea that you can be whole."

She's on to something important in understanding the sign in this story. Jesus introduces a changed story line, one that has the man getting up and walking away. What Jesus brings to the situation is a perspective that shifts the story from what the man doesn't have to what he has: the desire and means to get up.

I hear an empathetic tone in Jesus's question, "Do you want to get well?" Jesus said to the man, "Get up! Pick up your mat and walk." Jesus doesn't lean over the man and pull him close to the water and offer to wait with him until it is stirred. He replaces the "I don't have what I need" story with the "Use your strength to get up and carry your mat" story. It is as if Jesus is saying to the man, "Do you have a vision for not sitting by this pool? Pick up your mat and carry it."

Calling People off Their Mats by Calling Them onto a Mat

People all over the world are doing this kind of work in helping people to find new stories so they can be freed from the limiting bondages keeping them down. This is what you would see if you went to the OakFit gym outside of Dallas, Texas. It is a unique kind of gymnasium run by David Vobora. The gym provides free personalized physical training programs for injured veterans and people living with disabilities as a way to fulfill its mission: "To empower the human athlete, restore hope through movement, and redefine the limits of individuals with disabilities."

A picture of what they do there is seen in the relationship between David Vobora and Brian Aft. The two met when Brian was living on the street trying to manage the devastating effects of his heroin addiction. Aft is a marine veteran and a double amputee who lost both legs from a roadside bomb in Afghanistan in 2011. Like so many people whose addiction to painkillers leads them to heroin use, Aft was on the street. One day Vobora drove by in his car and saw him, and recognized in him something familiar.

Vobora is a former NFL linebacker whose own life went off the rails due to his addiction to the painkillers he was prescribed to manage a shoulder injury. Vobora slammed on his breaks, jumped out of his car, ran up to Aft, and said, "I'm David Vobora, a former NFL player. What happened?" Aft told his story, and Vobora invited him to join him in his gym in order to find his life again and to change his future.

Aft had been a strong, self-reliant marine and felt he had lost himself and was no longer the man he once was. Vobora knew this same sense of loss after leaving football and becoming addicted to painkillers. So this invitation to come to the gym came from a man who knew what it meant to get well.

An article in *ESPN Magazine* describes the scene in the gym. "They form a loose circle, some sitting in wheelchairs, others in folding chairs, with their prosthetic legs or arms stretched out in front. A few, with their prosthetics removed, rest on their stumps on the floor. Others stand, holding crutches or leaning on gym equipment. A quadruple amputee sits next to a triple amputee. A car crash survivor with no legs sits beside a veteran with one arm and one leg. Two quadriplegics confer with a single-leg amputee. They're all here, at OakFit gym on a rundown street outside of Dallas' downtown."[2]

Vobora and Aft describe what is happening at OakFit gym as more than just adapted physical training. People are getting new stories and new solutions. They are pulling, rolling, lifting, pushing, growing in mind and body. They are "walking again."

Religion That Benefits People, Not the Other Way Around

In this gospel story, our narrator is quick to add that this happened on the Sabbath. Jesus comes under considerable criticism in this story because he performs this healing on that day. Not only is the story about a person with a new perspective and a new ability to walk, it is about unraveling power structures that keep people down.

The Jewish religious leaders of Jesus's day were committed to keeping the Sabbath. And for good reason. The Sabbath was rooted in the story of the Hebrew faith right from the beginning. Unlike many of the religious laws of the day that were from the time of Moses, the keeping of the Sabbath went all the way back to the creation narrative. The Hebrew people included a day of rest in their creation narrative to underline the importance they already believed the Sabbath to have. In the faith, keeping the Sabbath was necessary because even God rested on the Sabbath. "On the sixth day God completed all the work that he had done, and on the seventh day God rested from all the work that he had done. God blessed the seventh day and made it holy, because on it God rested from all the work of creation" (Gen. 2:2–3).

You can see how a people who wanted themselves to be "holy" would want to honor a day that was made holy because

God rested on it. The Jewish leaders understood that this was not a literal resting of God; they understood that this creation story was showing that the Sabbath was a special and holy day. They understood, as we would, the use of anthropomorphic language around God to give something meaning. And that was just the point. This was a day that should be kept holy, and people should "be like God" and rest on that day. So, over the centuries there was considerable debate and clarity sought about what constituted work and what meant rest.

Jesus seems to be picking a fight with the Sabbath-keeping requirement all the way through the Gospels—as he said, the Sabbath was made for the benefit of humanity, humans were not made to keep the Sabbath. Jesus responds to the religious leaders who object to his doing this healing on the Sabbath, saying, "*My Father is still working, and I am working too*" (John 5:17). Here we see Jesus referring to these works, arguing that he is the one who is in line with the actions of God, who is always working, creating, making a new humanity.

The response of the leaders is to turn against Jesus and want to kill him. The text gives the reason for this violent response: "Not only because he was doing away with the Sabbath but also because he called God his own Father, thereby making himself equal with God" (John 5:18).

So, on that day when Jesus said, "Get up! Pick up your mat and walk," there was a significant double meaning. Jesus was saying that the man was freed from his limitations and no longer had to sit on the mat and that, because this work of God was done on the Sabbath, the people no longer had to fear that there are some days when God is not on their side.

Did Jesus have a twinkle in his eye when he released this man from the story he was trapped in—that there are rules to when and how you can be healed, whether it's about the timing to get in the water or having the right people to help get you in the water. There is nothing more important than the healing of a person. This is a greater-than work that people are doing today, freeing people from the limitations that some places or days are set aside for religious purposes at the expense of people themselves.

Pick Up and Walk

In addition to the broad implications of Jesus's work, we cannot overlook that the man was able to walk afterward. People are continuing to do work in human sciences in the most amazing ways. The significant advancements in biology, cell regeneration, transplants, artificial limbs, implants, and the like over the last century are mind-blowing. And there is no indication that this is slowing anytime soon.

By our modern standards, this story of making someone well so he can walk seems to be the most repeatable of all the miraculous signs. We have gotten really good at helping people walk. The group called the Amputee Coalition (www.amputee -coalition.org) takes the history of prosthetics back not only to the first patent for the "artificial leg" on November 4, 1846,[3] but to the ancient Egyptians. In an article called "A Brief History of Prosthesis," we learn that "the prosthetic field has morphed into a sophisticated example of man's determination to do better."[4]

The Walk Again Project is an international collaborative effort involving more than one hundred researchers. They built a system that allowed Juliano Pinto, who was paralyzed below the chest, to attend the ceremonial ball at the opening of the 2014 FIFA World Cup. They strapped Pinto inside a robotic exoskeleton and connected a "brain-machine interface" (BMI) that allowed him to control the exoskeleton with his thoughts.[5]

As impressive as it is to control a custom-fitted robotic device, an indication of the even more miraculous-sounding work being done in the area of neuroengineering can be seen in the title of an abstract from the *Journal of NeuroEngineering and Rehabilitation*: "The Feasibility of a Brain-Computer Interface Functional Electrical Stimulation System for the Restoration of Overground Walking after Paraplegia."[6] The article describes that through the proof-of-concept study, it is feasible to restore brain-controlled overground walking after damage to the spine. This means that spinal-cord stimulation can allow a person to voluntarily move his or her lower extremities by intuitive and direct brain control.

In 2015 a twenty-six-year-old man who had been paralyzed for five years due to a damaged spine did that very thing. The man wore an electrode cap that sent brain waves wirelessly to a computer that deciphered the waves and passed the intention to a microcontroller on his belt, which then triggered the nerves to move the muscles in his legs. He was able to walk just over ten feet using his own legs.[7] The possibility of allowing persons with damaged spines to control their legs with their own brain waves is, in my book, one of those greater-than accomplishments.

The amazing work continues in ways that must feel as miraculous to us as the work of Jesus did to people in the first century. Through development in stem cell research, it's only a matter of time before we know how to help our bodies generate limbs and organs when they are needed. There is great promise in the area of using mathematical algorithms to create therapies that allow people to grow organs and limbs. As totally mind-blowing as that may sound, researchers from the Duke-NUS Medical School in Singapore, the University of Bristol in the United Kingdom, Monash University in Australia, and RIKEN in Japan have published their work in the journal *Nature Genetics*.[8] We have gone far beyond the healing and wholeness environment and have entered the fantastical world of allowing the body to regenerate limbs and organs.

This kind of thing may frighten you just a bit and give you cause to find solidarity with the religious leaders of Jesus's day who accused him of trying to equate himself with God as you wonder if we have crossed some of the predetermined limits of humanity. I don't see it that way. I think we're just getting started on the greater works that are possible.

ABUNDANCE

That Time the Kid Showed There Was Enough

After this Jesus went across the Galilee Sea (that is, the Tiberias Sea). A large crowd followed him, because they had seen the miraculous signs he had done among the sick. Jesus went up a mountain and sat there with his disciples. It was nearly time for Passover, the Jewish festival.

Jesus looked up and saw the large crowd coming toward him. He asked Philip, "Where will we buy food to feed these people?" Jesus said this to test him, for he already knew what he was going to do.

Philip replied, "More than a half year's salary worth of food wouldn't be enough for each person to have even a little bit."

One of his disciples, Andrew, Simon Peter's brother, said, "A youth here has five barley loaves and two fish. But what good is that for a crowd like this?"

Jesus said, "Have the people sit down." There was plenty of grass there. They sat down, about five thousand of them. Then Jesus took the bread. When he had given thanks, he distributed it to those who were sitting there. He did the same with the fish, each getting as much as they wanted. When they had plenty to eat, he said to his disciples,

"Gather up the leftover pieces, so that nothing will be wasted." So they gathered them and filled twelve baskets with the pieces of the five barley loaves that had been left over by those who had eaten.

When the people saw that he had done a miraculous sign, they said, "This is truly the prophet who is coming into the world." Jesus understood that they were about to come and force him to be their king, so he took refuge again, alone on a mountain.

John 6:1–15

The feeding of thousands of people on the hillside is one of the most famous stories in the entire Jesus repertoire. If you're near your phone, tablet, or computer, search "Feeding the 5000." You will see that the power of this miracle story strikes deep into people's imaginations. Not only do people use the imagery in their names, Feedingthe5000.net, for example, but people also take the actions of the story seriously as they engage in work to feed the hungry.

One organization that caught my eye was FeedbackGlobal .org, which describes its "Feeding the 5000" work this way: "Feeding the 5000 is our flagship campaigning event to shine a light on the global food waste scandal, champion the delicious solutions and catalyse the global movement. At each event, we serve up a delicious communal feast for 5000 people made entirely out of food that would otherwise have been wasted."[1]

There are scores of organizations that use the details of the gospel story to give imagination and context for their work. The church I work at partners with an organization called Loaves and Fishes. Every other month we provide the daily meal for nearly 350 people in the basement of Holy Rosary Church. As far as I know, this group has never prepared a fish and bread dinner, but this story is certainly a great frame for us to understand what we are doing.

Part of what makes the feeding of the five thousand a popular story is that we live in a time when the production of food outpaces our ability to consume it all. We don't have a food production problem in the world, and there is more than enough food for everyone. We have a distribution problem. In fact, there is often too much capacity to grow food in some places and too little food in other places. In recent years obesity has proven to be as big a cause of death and health issues as malnutrition.[2]

This has not always been the case. Just one hundred years ago the problem facing the world was not having enough food resources. In fact, fifty years ago, futurists were terrified that the planet would not offer sufficient resources to feed the ever-expanding human population. Those fears have proven unfounded, but few people could have known that in the 1960s. And that is good news considering that we will need to produce more food in the next one hundred years than we have produced in the previous ten thousand years. So, in the approaching 2020s, we could do and outdo the miracle of providing food for thousands of people. People are finding new ways to distribute food, grow food, and enhance the health benefits of food across the world.

In so many ways, this miraculous sign is a story about providing food to those in need. However, as with all these signs, something even more significant is being pointed to: the use of people as providers of the needed food. And that is as true in the twenty-first century as it was in the first century.

Four particulars of this story stand out to me. One, it is a story built on other stories. It is framed as "after this" and "because they had seen the miraculous signs he had done among the sick." Together, these stories build a framework. The centurion came because he had heard something about Jesus. And the narrator of this story places it in Galilee, the place where Jesus turned water into wine.

This is a good reminder that the scenes in this story are connected with previous scenes, and we should see them as part of the same mosaic of the life of a new humanity and not as merely independent miracle stories. They are telling a large story of the creation of a new way. This connected holism resonates with something that is true in many of our lives. It can be easy to break our lives into sections and pieces and analyze each as its own experience. But there is something more whole, more beautiful in seeing our lives as a singularly connected expression. All the parts are part of the whole story.

Two, this story has its own dynamic in that it is the only "crowd miracle" in the Gospel of John. All the other miracles involve a single person as the beneficiary, with a small number of people even knowing what happened. This one is all about the crowd. In fact, that is exactly what this story tells us: there is something about the power of the "all."

Three, it is the only miracle in the Gospel where Jesus uses another person as a coconspirator. Not only is this a crowd miracle, but it's also a crowd-sourced miracle, the only miracle in John where Jesus uses the action of another person in the miraculous sign. In this case, it was the young boy who had enough.

This wasn't a miraculous sign that showed how a boy was given the food he needed; it was meant to catch everyone else up to this boy's situation of having enough. The boy is the supplier of that which was needed. This is a critical part of the story—the young, the marginalized, the one who seemed to be of no use at all in meeting the problem at hand was the star of the story.

The hinge of this story is set up at the start. As with all the miraculous signs in John, this one is told so that readers can imagine the scene. The word pictures are memorable. There is a huge crowd looking at the newest miracle worker expecting him to verify the rumors they had heard. You can almost feel the tension. Would he perform up to expectations? They are there to see what he would do next. It is at this moment that Jesus flips the story and brings one of them into focus as the star of the show.

As you get into the details of this story, you see that the whole thing feels like it was a setup: "Jesus said this to test him, for he already knew what he was going to do." The other miracle signs have the sense of Jesus almost stumbling into the situation—he doesn't want to be outed at a wedding; the soldier approaches him; he comes across one man of many at the pool. But in this story, Jesus seemingly creates the context to make a point. It is as if Jesus carries out this entire miracle as a piece of performance art.

"Jesus looked up and saw the large crowd coming toward him. He asked Philip, 'Where will we buy food to feed these people?' Jesus said this to test him, for he already knew what he was going to do." Jesus asked Philip a question in order to test him. A lot can hinge on how we read the term "to test." It can easily sound like Jesus was trying to find fault with Philip. Or just the opposite: Jesus was trying to open his mind. Instead of seeing this crowd as the problem, Philip was invited to see it as part of the solution.

Where will *we* buy enough food? If the disciple is thinking of himself as the supplier and the masses as the recipients, this is a good question. And Philip, the unknowing patsy in this lesson of abundance, answers as many of us would: we don't have anywhere near enough resources. "More than a half year's salary worth of food wouldn't be enough for each person to have even a little bit."

This is the very way of thinking that Jesus is looking to change. The narrator lets us, the readers, in on the story. "Jesus said this to test him, for he already knew what he was going to do." This is not a story of coming up with enough food from diminishing resources. This is a story of seeing that there is enough among the people already.

The powerful imagery in this story might not be as obvious to a modern reader as it would have been to someone of the first century: the boy was carrying more than a typical amount of daily food; he had an abundance. It might not seem obvious to us at first glance, but the noting of five loaves and two fish was an indicator that this kid was packing. This is a story about seeing the abundance that exists. It is testing whether we will see the world through a lens of scarcity or one of abundance. It is a story that wants to extend the story of a daily provision and to ask people to be the instigators of a sharing and abundance way of life. A friend of mine puts it this way: "At that time it would have most commonly been assumed that people would have had their own food for the day. But it was the disciples who didn't have food and assumed other people were in the same situation. So, the boy becomes an example of the sharing economy."

Four, this story is deeply connected to the broader Hebrew story. This is a provision story, and one that sits in contrast to the Hebrew people's most famous provision story of manna from heaven. In this story, it is a young boy from whom the provision comes. It is not a dew settling over the people in a mysterious way, and it is far more mundane and far more beautiful—a boy has enough.

As with so many of these stories, the location plays an integral part in understanding the sign. This story is set on a hillside. And people are in need of food. This story is set up to reflect on the narrative of the nation of Israel during their exodus from Egypt. In the Hebrew story, the exodus was part of the making of the people, where they came from, what they went through, and who they are now. They were led from Egypt by Moses to the promised land. They were called to leave behind the practices and mind-sets of being slaves in Egypt to become free people in the promised land of Israel. This journey took an entire generation, forty years, and meant going through the wilderness places. God provided for them on this journey with manna from heaven. An essential part of their story is that God, and not their slaveholders, provided.

The people on this journey were having a hard time making the transition from their old life as slaves to their new life as wanderers. Any of us who have had to make significant life transitions can understand why Exodus would tell the story that way. So often change can be hard.

The text of Exodus 16 says the people were complaining to Moses about their new situation in the wilderness: "Oh, how we wish that the LORD had just put us to death while we were still in the land of Egypt. There we could sit by the pots cooking meat and eat our fill of bread. Instead, you've brought us out into this desert to starve this whole assembly to death" (Exod. 16:3).

What all the people in this story could see was that there was not enough. The story goes on to describe what happens next. And it is nearly impossible to miss the parallels to our story of Jesus on the hillside, just before the Passover celebration: "Then the LORD said to Moses, 'I'm going to make bread rain down from the sky for you. The people will go out each day and gather just enough for that day. In this way, I'll test them to see whether or not they follow my Instruction. On the sixth day, when they measure out what they have collected, it will be twice as much as they collected on other days'" (Exod. 16:4–5).

In the Exodus story, the Lord puts together a plan where there is enough for just one day, and then on the sixth day there will be a double portion, enough for the seventh day. This story is told to show how vital keeping the Sabbath was. No need to provide on the seventh day; there was enough for two days given on the sixth day. The story goes on to say that "in the morning there was a layer of dew all around the camp. When the layer of dew lifted, there on the desert surface were thin flakes, as thin as frost on the ground. . . . The Israelite people called it manna. It was like coriander seed, white, and tasted like honey wafers" (Exod. 16:13–14, 31). The parallels are obvious: there is a need, there is a test, there is a sense there is not enough, there is more given than needed.

In this retelling of an Exodus story, Jesus's test is to see if Philip and others will see the provisions given for this new way of humanity Jesus is announcing. In the new humanity it is not that there is only enough for one day; there is more than people can eat, there is an abundance. There is not only extra on the seventh day; every day is a Sabbath-like day of abundance. As the signs build through the Gospel of John, we see Jesus demonstrate that the new humanity can live in the Sabbath freedom in all places and times without it being managed by the temple system.

Meeting Food Needs

We should not miss the fact that feeding 7 billion people on our planet is already a miracle. As unacceptable as it is that people are going hungry, it is incredible that we can feed as many people as we do. If current population growth predictions are accurate, there will be 9.7 billion people on the planet by 2050.[3] To put that in perspective, at the time of Jesus there were approximately 300 million people on the earth.[4] That is fewer people than in the United States of America today. The population of the planet has grown at an incredible pace, passing the 1 billion mark in 1804 and reaching more than 7.6 billion by 2010.

This rate of increase is likely to continue, which has an enormous impact on how much food will be needed. Consider this incredible statistic: in fifty years we will need to produce more food in one year than was produced in the last thousand years combined! This may sound terrifying, but it is also doable. And, ironically, finding success in this field will also provide the needed changes in our food system that will supply what is required to save our planet from climate change and to ensure food security for people around the globe.

The current global food structure is too water-intensive, too limited to the wealthy, too restricted by governments and dictators, too wasteful and oppressive. For all the success seen in aeroponics, hydroponics, bug-resistant crops, and the use of solar power, hydropower, and wind power for production, it's the increase in small-farm sustainability that will allow for food to grow in the places where people live.

Currently, there are specific "bread baskets" around the world. The food grown in those places needs to be transported to the areas where the people are. The fact that in the current agriculture economy it is only financially viable for large farming conglomerates to make food on a global scale means that the power will stay with certain people. However, people working in the science, social organizing, and technology fields are showing a way forward that will allow for smaller farms, local economies, and more calorie-, vitamin-, and mineral-rich food.

Work is being done to make nutritionally dense food available to people everywhere in the world. This food also must be made available in more places and production of it placed in the hands of more people. *National Geographic* describes the five steps that must be taken to feed, over the next twenty-five years, what is expected to be a population of nine billion people with a diet that will allow all people to thrive.[5]

Step 1: Freeze Agriculture's Footprint
National Geographic explains, "For most of history, whenever we've needed to produce more food, we've simply cut down forests or plowed grasslands to make more farms. . . . But we can no longer afford to increase food production through agricultural expansion." In the future, more of the right food will need to be produced from a shrinking agricultural footprint, and this will mean increased productivity. This leads to step 2.

Step 2: Grow More on the Farms We've Got
Significant advances in "high-tech, precision farming systems, as well as approaches borrowed from organic farming," accordgin to *National Geographic,* "could boost yields in these places several times over."

Step 3: Use Resources More Efficiently
Farmers are improving soil quality, saving water, and enhancing nutrients through composting and using cover crops and mulches. This is happening in both small farms and large commercial operations. Farmers also use water more intelligently; they use advanced sensors on their equipment to effectively spread fertilizers and pesticides; and they use location technology (GPS) to target treatment based on soil conditions, which increases yields and reduces runoff. This all produces what is referred to as "more crop per drop" outcomes. These outcomes have already made an enormous difference.

Step 4: Shift Our Diets

As *National Geographic* puts it, "It would be far easier to feed nine billion people by 2050 if more of the crops we grew ended up in human stomachs. Today only 55 percent of the world's crop calories feed people directly; the rest is fed to livestock (about 36 percent) or turned into biofuels and industrial products (roughly 9 percent)."

This is where new approaches to raising meat coupled with meatless diets are likely to play a significant role in feeding the world's population. As creepy as it sounds to some, meat grown in laboratories might play a significant role in feeding people and saving precious resources and ultimately saving the planet by protecting forests and grasslands.

Step 5: Reduce Waste

According to *National Geographic*, "An estimated 25 percent of the world's food calories and up to 50 percent of total food weight are lost or wasted before they can be consumed. In rich countries most of that waste occurs in homes, restaurants, or supermarkets. In poor countries food is often lost between the farmer and the market, due to unreliable storage and transportation." Excellent work is being done in this area, and eating habits are being changed in rich countries and refrigeration systems are being improved in poorer countries.

All five steps outlined by *National Geographic* are occurring right now, being accomplished by businesses, nonprofits, government organizations, and nongovernment entities. Miraculous levels of food are being made available because of the work of scientists, social organizers, farmers, engineers, and individuals making personal choices.

The people at Feedback, in their cleverly named organization, encourage people to give their excess food to those who can use it. They claim that three billion people in the world could be fed by food already in the system that is normally wasted.

Throughout their website they suggest four specific practices through which the food industry could make a profound difference.[6]

1. *Properly labeled dates.* Supermarkets and manufacturers should replace the confusing "best if used by," "sell by," "expires on," and other labels that lead to consumers unknowingly throwing out good food.
2. *Ugly vegetables.* Supermarkets should sell "ugly" fruit and vegetables and stop causing farmers and suppliers to waste perfectly good food on account of overly strict cosmetic buying policies.
3. *Transparency casserole.* Supermarkets and major manufacturers should measure and report precisely how much food they currently waste, as hiding the problem hinders the solutions.
4. *Just desserts.* Supermarkets and food retailers should make all unsold, surplus, fit-for-consumption food available to organizations that can put it to good use by feeding people, rather than just discarding it.

People who want to use the excess of their lives for goodness and to help others capture the spirit and calling of the miraculous sign.

"Until All Are Fed"

"We mean it when we say it: 'We want to reach everyone until ALL are fed.' Because no one deserves to go hungry, *especially* when we can do something about it." That is how the people at Feed My Starving Children (FMSC) describe their work. Not just a motto or organizational goal, this statement is taken personally by the people at FMSC. And they invite people to participate personally. According to their website, "The work we do is deeply personal to us, our volunteers, donors, food distribution partners and meal recipients. . . . We've worked hard to create nutritious meal formulas that really meet the need of starving people, and this food makes a real impact in their lives."[7]

In the early 1990s a team of eight food scientists from Cargill, Pillsbury, and General Mills developed a fortified rice formula rich in protein and micronutrients that was simple to prepare, could be stored in many conditions, and was designed uniquely for malnourished children. The ingredients are delivered in food packs that, when combined with water, make nutritious meals that are also vegetarian and halal-certified. This makes them culturally neutral and acceptable to populations worldwide. It was a fantastic accomplishment. Their work has saved and improved the lives of millions. The work continues with new food designed to help mothers of infants as well as children.

I first heard about this from Ann Hill, who works with Feed My Starving Children. Ann knows the details of hunger around the world. She has been in the villages and has seen food shortage needs firsthand. And she has met those needs. She is a modern-day miracle worker. Ann says there are three levels of food shortage: hunger, malnourishment, and starvation. Feed My Starving Children is a prevent-starvation effort.

One time when Ann was in Africa talking with a mother who was nursing a baby, the woman's two-year-old daughter came up to the mother, indicating that she wanted to nurse too. The mother scolded the two-year-old and said she was frustrated with her because "she knows that it is not her day to eat." Ann was heartbroken at the terrible position this sweet woman was in—having to ration her breast milk because she could not produce sufficient milk for both of her children due to her nutritional deficit.

This far-too-common situation is what has propelled FMSC to create a food pack called Potato W, where the *W* stands for "weaning." It is specially formulated for nursing mothers. One of the best ways to build health in children is to ensure that their mothers are healthy when nursing.

Feed My Starving Children has made a commitment not only to providing life-changing food but also to engaging as many people as possible in the work of getting this food delivered. In 2017 they packed and delivered 310 million meals, allowing nearly 3 million people to receive a year's worth of food. And they did it as an almost entirely volunteer organization.

Their model is to invite people into the packing and distribution process. The wonderful thing about the way FMSC operates is that they engage individuals, school groups, community groups, and churches in the packing and delivery of the food packets. In 2017, 1.2 million volunteers participated in the packing of the meals. That makes FMSC among the largest volunteer organizations in the world. Through the help of volunteers, their cost per meal, from food production to consumer, is twenty-two cents.

Ann tells me that they could deliver more food at a lower price and more efficiently if they outsourced the packing to a processing company to automate it. But they are sure that in the long run, that would lead to less money for the effort. When people are engaged in the process, they become involved in the outcome and are willing to fund the effort. When people help, they give. When they give, they care. Sure, there are times when it works the other way: first people care, then they give, then they help. But that is the rare case. What FMSC knows is that people care and invest in projects and efforts that allow for their full participation.

Asking people to put their hands on the packages and to place them in deliverable containers is not only about efficiency, it is also about engaging people in the process of helping others. This is what we see in the story of the feeding of the five thousand. The boy's fish, the disciples' care, the people's need are all part of the story.

FEARLESSNESS

That Time on the Lake

When evening came, Jesus' disciples went down to the lake. They got into a boat and were crossing the lake to Capernaum. It was already getting dark and Jesus hadn't come to them yet. The water was getting rough because a strong wind was blowing. When the wind had driven them out for about three or four miles, they saw Jesus walking on water. He was approaching the boat and they were afraid. He said to them, "I Am. Don't be afraid." Then they wanted to take him into the boat, and just then the boat reached the land where they had been heading.

John 6:16–21

This fifth miraculous sign is the most provocative of the entire set of seven. It carries the allure of spectacle with it. There is something in our human experience that does not want to settle for the limits of nature, and this story gets to the heart of that desire.

A few years ago my wife, Shelley, forwarded me a link to a video of men running on water for nearly one hundred feet. It was a three-minute documentary-style video made by a Portuguese shoe company introducing a new sport they created called "liquid mountaineering." They purport to have developed a means by which people can run on water by using their specially designed water-repellent shoes. It's an engaging video and genius in many ways.

Using an interview-style format, they overlay footage of person after person running on the surface of a lake as the founder of the company explains the "science" that makes all this possible. They go into detail describing how they used what has been learned about the speed and curvature of rocks from skipping stones to develop special shoes and a technique that allows a person to stay on top of the water propelled by just his or her body. Hence, liquid mountaineering.

"It takes a lot of practice, a lot of focus. I think that if you don't actually believe you are going to walk on that water, it is not going to happen for you," the founder says in an upbeat, encouraging tone. It was this statement, on the power of belief, that inspired my wife to send me the video. The desire to have what we believe in our hearts and minds make a difference in our physical reality is compelling for many people.

And it's inspiring when you first see it. The video shows people running on a grassy shore to gain speed, and when they enter the water, they just keep going an impressively long distance, sometimes thirty yards, until they lose momentum and sink into the water. If you have ever run into a lake or ocean, you know that the water stops all forward motion after just a few steps.

The video includes slow-motion footage of person after person running on top of the water and concludes with the founder commenting in English (with a Portuguese accent adding flair and intrigue): "People want you to think only in a certain way, but this sport allows you to push your horizons further. It is not boxing you in and saying, that's what you are. You are moving past it all." It is powerful seeing people do something incredible while a person tells you that our false limits can be dropped at the water's edge.

As soon as I saw the title of the video, "Walk on Water (Liquid Mountaineering)," I was suspicious. Even before watching, I looked up "running on water hoax" online.

Bingo.

The entire project was designed by the Hi-Tec Shoe Company to get people to do just what I did, assume the video was a hoax and start looking for proof. The search led me to another video, "Making of Hi-Tec Liquid Mountaineering." It turns out this is just what Hi-Tec wanted me to find. In the "Making of . . ." video, the marketing team for the company explains how they wanted to attract attention for their water-repellent shoe by creating a viral video where they could introduce their shoe and reveal how they made it appear that people were running on water.

Footage revealed a sophisticated custom floating dock that sat just below the water and moved with each step, giving an illusion of being on top of the water. The video included interviews about the making of the initial video.

"What are we doing here?" the person behind the camera asks.

"Selling the world a new sport," the runner says with a chuckle.

"Why?"

"Because the world needs something to believe in," he replies with a friendly smirk.

This clever strategy for a start-up shoe company targeted at young people looking for water-repellent shoes takes advantage of both the power of people wanting to overcome limits and the impulse to expose a hoax.

More than 750,000 people have watched "Making of Hi-Tec Liquid Mountaineering" and learned about this shoe. The thing is, that first video about running on water has been viewed over fifteen million times on YouTube. Why the difference in viewing rates? People don't want their sense of wonder and possibility disproved.

When sharing these videos in presentations with groups, I have discovered that the explanation video does not match the power of the running-on-water video. There is a kind of "I knew it was possible" excitement in the air when people see the runners staying on top of the water. On some occasions, people have even excitedly applauded at the end of the video. And I feel a bit sadistic preparing them for the collective shoulder slump of disappointment as the true story unfolds.

The Desire to Overcome Limits and Live in Harmony

There's a powerful desire in the human spirit to overcome natural limits. At least in part, human evolution has created that desire. As a species, we have tracked across continents, crossed oceans, and climbed over mountain ranges. We have learned to fly machines and have shot rockets to the moon. We seek to cure illnesses, to understand what is at the bottom of the ocean and in the farthest galaxies.

The passion for human beings to overcome the perceived limits of nature is built into our evolutionary development. We are a species that has developed by finding ways to survive by being protected from the natural world and overcoming its limits. Humanity has overcome natural threats that range from storms to animals, from viruses to falling trees, from water that can swallow us up to water that rushes down hillsides with the force of an avalanche. Human beings are nature survivors. This is what makes the "nature" miracles of Jesus so interesting. Something in them seems connected to our human desire for survival. It is part of our very relationship with nature. We need a relationship with nature that allows not only for human thriving but also for the thriving of all living things. This is what the walking-on-water story compels us toward.

As attractive as it might be to see Jesus not limited by the confines of nature, the essential question is, "What is the miraculous sign done here?" We might answer, it's obvious of course: Jesus walked on the top of the water! And as far as the "memorable miracles" of Jesus, this undoubtedly ranks near the top of the list. But at first glance, there doesn't seem to be any benefit to this miracle. It comes across as a demonstration of power or a great ability, but what is the sign that it points to? It seems to lack a beneficiary. Where's the good news in this one-off power display that no one can repeat?

I've begun to believe that, in the same way the liquid mountaineering video leads viewers to another video, this story is designed to point the reader to an important pathway of greater empathy, emotional maturity, and well-being for humanity.

The Inverted Story

This story hinges as much on the words used as on the actions performed. Jesus says only five words in the story, but they sit at its center: "I Am. Don't be afraid." They stand alongside the narrator's description of the action: "When the wind had driven them out for about three or four miles, they saw Jesus walking on water. He was approaching the boat and they were afraid. He said to them, 'I Am. Don't be afraid.'"

Jesus's use of the expression "I Am" plays a significant role in the Gospel of John. It is a particular use rooted in the name of the Hebrew God and has an enormous impact on how we are to understand Jesus and what story the Gospel of John is telling. Some people have concluded that Jesus's use of the term was his way of claiming divinity. Since the term was used in the Hebrew Bible as the title for God, they conclude that Jesus was using it to refer to himself as God. But Jesus here seems to deliberately use that term for a different reason.

In the book of Exodus, we're introduced to Moses as the leader chosen to free the Israelites from their slavery in Egypt. In that story, Moses will lead those Israelites across the sea by parting the waters. Then Moses goes up on a mountain and engages with God and there receives the tablets with the Ten Commandments that serve as a covenant between God and the people. These people will be fed and kept alive by manna from heaven.

Maybe you already see the parallels to John's Gospel: God's chosen leader; providing food for the people; a mountain trek; a water event. Jesus is the new Moses.

The "I Am" statement comes from the Moses story as well. At the start of this Exodus story, Moses seeks to convince the Israelite people that he is indeed a God-sent leader.

> But Moses said to God, "If I now come to the Israelites and say to them, 'The God of your ancestors has sent me to you,' they are going to ask me, 'What's this God's name?' What am I supposed to say to them?"
>
> God said to Moses, "I Am Who I Am. So say to the Israelites, 'I Am has sent me to you.'" God continued,

"Say to the Israelites, 'The LORD, the God of your ancestors, Abraham's God, Isaac's God, and Jacob's God, has
sent me to you.' This is my name forever; this is how all
generations will remember me." (Exod. 3:13–15)

When Jesus uses the "I Am" and "Do not be afraid" phrases,
you can see this carrying the power of the entire Moses story.
What the Gospel of John does with this sign is tell an inverted
version of the story of the exodus.

In the walking-on-water scene, Jesus and the disciples are
not leaving Egypt for Israel with Jerusalem at the center. They
are leaving *from* Jerusalem *to* enter the area of Capernaum.
And as we've seen before, the signs interrelate. This water-
walking story connects to the previous feeding-the-multitude
story, where the provision did not come from heaven only but
also from one another. In this inverted exodus story, the waters
are not split for the safe passage of the Israelites, only to come
crashing on the Egyptians, bringing about their destruction.
This time the water is presented as something that can hold life
and needs not be feared.

The story of the exodus out of Egypt was the framing narrative for the Hebrew people for how they should live. It was, and
is, the basis of the Passover celebration. It framed the promises
of God and the call of the Hebrew people. It was the story a
people were called to remember and to emulate.

The walking-on-water story serves as a way for the people
of Jesus's way to understand their version of an exodus. We're
given an exodus by Jesus out of a mind-set of fear, superstition,
and anxiety.

A Water Worldview

Water is a key to this story. In fact, water plays an essential role in four of the seven signs: water to wine, the man wanting to get in the pool, walking on water, and the blind man washing in the pool. The use of water in the Gospel of John is prevalent and makes sense since water is so closely connected to human life. All humans need water to survive.

Water is literally everywhere. Seventy percent of the earth's surface is covered by it. And, as many of us were taught in elementary school, our bodies are 60 percent water. According to the US Geological Survey's Water Science School, that statistic undersells the significance of water to our bodies. They remind us that "the brain and heart are composed of 73% water, and the lungs are about 83% water. The skin contains 64% water, muscles and kidneys are 79%, and even the bones are watery: 31%."[1] Water is crucial and ubiquitous to human existence. We drink, breathe, and expel water; we also organize our lives around it. All civilizations on the planet have been built around water, be it a river, a well, a lake, or an ocean. Humans came from water, are made of water, and have always remained near water.

At the same time, over the course of history, humans have also feared water and have given it a near-mythical level of power. For much of human history, how the earth, the winds, and water work has been foreign and mysterious. This lack of understanding coupled with respect for the power of the elements has contributed to people living in fear of water.

In the ancient world, "the water of the sea" represented chaos, danger, evil. Not evil in the sense of moral wrong, but evil in the sense of dread and destruction. It is in this context that we find the significance of Jesus walking on water—it is not merely to be understood as overcoming the physical nature of water but as overcoming the sense of danger and chaos the water represents. Jesus not being afraid of, or at the whim of, the sea is part of the new creation story the Gospel of John tells.

A New Creation Story

Again, the Gospel of John finds a rhythm with the opening poem of the book of Genesis. That creation story uses the imagery of the water and seas as places of brooding darkness and chaos. "When God began to create the heavens and the earth—the earth was without shape or form, it was dark over the deep sea, and God's wind swept over the waters" (Gen. 1:1–2).

One of the first acts in this creation story is making life in the midst of the "deep sea." "God said, 'Let the waters under the sky come together into one place so that the dry land can appear'" (Gen. 1:9). Then "God said, 'Let the waters swarm with living things'" (Gen. 1:20).

Then the story turns to the people God made and calls them to live without fear of the sea, but rather to have charge over it: "God blessed them and said to them, 'Be fertile and multiply; fill the earth and master it. Take charge of the fish of the sea'" (Gen. 1:28).

The creation story in the book of Genesis served ancient Israel as an alternative to the competing creation stories of other cultures of early Mesopotamia. Those creation stories tended to center on gods using nature to punish humanity. The God of Genesis calls people not to fear but to live as partners with the earth and the sea. To care for it, to engage in it, to find life in all parts of it, from the land to the air and even in the midst of the deep sea. In this story, humans are to be as deeply connected to the earth and sea as they are to one another.

As we begin to discover, living in partnership with water rather than fearing it is what Jesus's walking-on-water story points to. "Do not fear the waters of the deep," the creation story tells us. This image of not fearing becomes an example for us, as it did for the disciples, of how to set aside our super-stitions, preconceived fears, and inhibitions of what is on the other side. This story uses the construct of crossing to the other side in a much broader sense than just moving the characters from one side of the lake to the other.

This is a story where the water, the deep, the chaos, the void are traversed, not feared. This is a story about making it safely to the other side even amid fears and superstitions.

The Emotional State of the Disciples

Another way in which this sign is different from the others is that we see it through the emotional state of the disciples. It is the disciples in the boat who are the beneficiaries in the story. This sign is not about a change in something external to the disciples but about a shift in their emotional state. In that way, this story is one of the most personal of the seven.

As we encounter the story, we are drawn into the emotional situation of the characters in the boat. This is a story where the dramas of life's struggle are in full view. We see the condition that the disciples are in. Five phrases from the story serve as our guide to see what this act of walking on water accomplished and teach us how we can engage with it in our own lives.

To provide a recap, here's the story again:

> When evening came, Jesus' disciples went down to the lake. They got into a boat and were crossing the lake to Capernaum. It was already getting dark and Jesus hadn't come to them yet. The water was getting rough because a strong wind was blowing. When the wind had driven them out for about three or four miles, they saw Jesus walking on water. He was approaching the boat and they were afraid. He said to them, "I Am. Don't be afraid." Then they wanted to take him into the boat, and just then the boat reached the land where they had been heading. (John 6:16–21)

The following five phrases open a sense of drama not only for the disciples but for most of us as human beings.

"When evening came" and "It was already getting dark"

These phrases (which we'll count as one phrase) let us know that this takes place at night—the only sign to do so. The disciples are in the dark, and they are on the water. If you have spent much time in the wilderness, you can understand how much energy goes into getting situated before night falls. It is tough for novices to navigate on a dark lake, something I've experienced firsthand. I've had to paddle hard and long on Boundary Waters lakes between the United States and Canada to get a group of high school students in our three canoes to a campsite before nightfall. No one wants to be stuck on a lake in the dark trying to find your way to the other side. When this story says that evening was coming and "it was already getting dark," we are drawn into a drama in which something is changing. Darkness is coming.

This sense of it getting dark is not only felt on a lake or in the wilderness at night. It is something that many people experience in the safety of their own beds at night, where fears, anxieties, and worries visit us. The time between "Good night" and "Good morning" can be among the most challenging. We even use this language of night to capture our fears or despondency; we describe people experiencing a "dark night of the soul" or feeling like they are in "some kind of darkness." And this is what we are to feel in this story: the human struggle when darkness is setting in.

This use of evening and darkness might be getting at something deeper than just a metaphor. There is significant work being done on the function of the brain's frontal lobe at different times of the day. When the brain is tired or low on food and resources, it tends not to do its work as well as when it is rested and well nourished.

The frontal lobe is responsible for complex thinking. When that part of our brain is not high functioning, the more base parts of the brain take over. Many of us know this anecdotally— we don't make good decisions when we are tired. We get crabby when we're hungry.

Neurologists pay significant attention to this in studies of people with Alzheimer's disease. They know people's memories are less accurate in the evenings, producing anxiety in people who suffer from the disease. The fact that fear responses in our brains are more intense as it gets late helps us understand that this story is about fear setting in, simply through the use of the phrases "When evening came" and "It was already getting dark."

The sense of clarity and vision lost or lessened has real-world implications. One study done with a large number of parole cases reveals how judges make decisions about who receives parole (as one example). Judges who made parole decisions just after lunch granted parole to inmates roughly 60 percent of the time. Judges hearing cases before lunch, presumably when they were hungry, granted parole almost 0 percent of the time.[2] When it's getting late, when they're getting hungry, when it's getting dark—in these moments, judges tended to be less empathic, less reasonable, and less willing to grant parole.

As people who are called to live with kindness, grace, and generosity, we can see what a threat it is to human thriving when we are short on food, water, or rest. In this condition, we are more likely to live in a survival mode dominated by fear and scarcity.

"Jesus hadn't come to them yet"

The story brings us back into the interior life of the disciples. As we meet this phrase, we feel the tension in the story mount as they get in a boat to cross the tumultuous sea to go to the other side—without their leader. They are on their own. They were being forced into something they weren't ready to do. We see the universal human experience of feeling stretched beyond our comfort, of moving into a lack of certainty and perhaps a lack of safety. Religious teachers, therapists, and psychologists, including the famed Abraham Harold Maslow, have stressed the impact of basic human needs being met on a person's sense of safety and well-being. It is crucial that human needs are met, and it is also important that people have a sense that those needs are met. In this story we see the power of the narrative of scarcity. As the story unfolds, it becomes apparent that the disciples indeed had all they needed to cross the lake. The story emphasizes this when Jesus "comes to them" and this perceived need is thereby fulfilled, for "just then the boat reached the land where they had been heading." They didn't need Jesus with them to make it to the other side. We see echoes of the previous events—the panic, the sense of there not being enough, the discovery that they had what they needed all along.

"The water was getting rough because a strong wind was blowing"

In the third set of anxiety-building factors, we see the story increase in intensity as the boat is now being driven by the wind, away from the shore by three or four miles, far from safety. The boat is not on its path and is at the mercy of the wind and waves. On the water or off, we connect this to human experience. We have a sense of urgency to get somewhere before nightfall, and the situation, the weather, the events conspire to leave us feeling that our lives are not going as we planned or desired. Other forces are driving us out, miles from home. The sense that we are rudderless at sea is a feeling familiar to many.

"They saw Jesus walking on water"

In this phrase we see a switch, an alternative to fear of the darkness. Jesus walked on water, a man who was not at the whim of the water or wind. One who was not being blown about by the elements but instead was walking where he wanted. And he walked more efficiently than the craft designed for the water, the boat, could take the disciples. The one who was in the very elements they feared was telling them they need not be afraid.

"They wanted to take him into the boat"

What we meet in this last phrase is the shift from anxiety to a clear, important, engaging, and understandable desire. If you believed the boat to be a place of safety, you would want to bring Jesus into it. But in this story, the boat is not a place of safety. All the action is in the water amid all the perceived chaos and danger.

The narrator makes clear that the disciples in the boat were fearful for Jesus on the water and wanted to save him. "They wanted to take him into the boat, and just then the boat reached the land where they had been heading." Just when fear was about to take over, it became clear that the water was not something Jesus needed to be saved from. He did not need the boat for protection from sinking into the deep, which we understand in Jesus saying, "I Am. Do not be afraid." This was the miraculous event: the removal of fear and getting to the place you were headed even in the midst of the storms you can't control.

The idea of living as those who cross to the other side connects with people all over the world. Sometimes our crossing involves moving from one place to another. At other times it means opening our hearts to the needs and struggles of others, crossing into their world, for their benefit and ours. We often need to overcome fear in our relationship with ourselves, engaging with our own scary memories and histories to move our lives forward.

The Power of Crossing to the Other Side

Water in this story represents not only fear but also a border. The other side of the lake has an "other side of the tracks" sense in this story.

My friend Kelly Bean, who operates a wonderful organization called African Road that creates partnerships between people from the United States and people on the continent of Africa, likes to say, "Sometimes we need to cross an ocean before we can cross the street." What she is getting at is something many of us know to be true. It is easy to get stuck in our safe places and routines, and it is really tough to break those patterns. Kelly has found that people often need to make a big step before they will make a small one.

Kelly serves as a modern-day water walker by helping people who have been taught over a lifetime to think of people from faraway places as strangers. Her way of assisting people to live beyond their fears of strange places and strange people is to get them right in the "water." She connects people over meals in huts, in cars as travel mates, and around community fires. She makes it possible for people on different sides of the globe to engage as friends who have gifts for each other. This practice, Kelly told me, leads to those same people being more confident and interested in finding their way across the street at home as well.

Empathy Is the Antidote to Separation and Fear

Empathy is a crucial quality that allows us as human beings to trust in and care about others. Human beings possess the ability for and are designed for empathy. It is our willingness to engage this capacity that allows us to live beyond our limited, fearful, more simplistic, base, animalistic way of engaging with one another. And empathy is at the heart of Jesus's "greater things than these" teaching. The call to empathy echoes Jesus's call for people to love one another as they love themselves. What Jesus calls for, and what John's Gospel presents as the image of a new humanity, is not some esoteric call for a new kind of superhuman but something our hearts, spirits, brains, and bodies are made for.

Jeremy Rifkin is an economist and social theorist with a great interest in why humans live the way they do. In his book *The Empathic Civilization*, he argues that we are "soft-wired" for experiencing another's plight as if it were our own. In a speech for the Royal Society for the Arts, he said, "We are soft-wired *not* for aggression, violence, self-interest, and utilitarianism. . . . We are soft-wired for sociability, attachment, affection, and companionship."[3]

According to Rifkin, our most primal human drive—belonging—is an empathic drive. We see this when babies hear another child crying; they experience the empathic drive, and they, in turn, start to cry. As people grow, they begin to understand themselves in relationship to others and that they can experience another's plight as if it were their own. We can find a connection to another's suffering and joy. This is what we see when we study the function of the human brain. And this is what we see when we look at human history and patterns.[4]

We also know that consciousness has changed. The human brain has developed over time, and our brains today are structured differently than human brains from the hunter-gatherer period some twenty-five thousand years ago. To "empathize is to civilize,"[5] Rifkin says. This is what we have been doing over the course of human history—extending our connection and empathy to increasingly broadening communities—or, to borrow a phrase from our story, "crossing to the other side."

Rifkin suggests that over the last ten thousand years, the human brain has developed in ways that have

allowed us to extend our sense of belonging from our familial/tribal/blood ties, to conceptual or theological ties that were made possible by the advent of script and developing transportation, which leads to religious ties. In the nineteenth century, a market-driven economy created a new economy where people living in the same country, regardless of blood ties or religion, became a new "us" to which one could belong. Brits, Germans, French began seeing one another as extended families, which allowed us to have loyalties and identities. The pattern that seems to grow and that many social theorists are excited to pursue is the idea that the entire human civilization could begin to see itself as one human family, sharing the entire biosphere with all living creatures.[6]

All this might seem out of sync with what we believe we know about human history, which appears to be the story of anything but empathy, inclusion, and crossing barriers to finding the "other." But Rifkin argues that history

is more often than not made by the disgruntled and discontented, the angry and rebellious—those interested in exercising authority and exploiting others and their victims, interested in righting wrongs and restoring justice. By this reckoning, much of history is about the pathology of power. Perhaps that is why, when we come to think about human nature, we have such a bleak analysis. Our collective memory is measured in terms of crises and calamities, harrowing injustices, and terrifying episodes of brutality inflicted on each other and our fellow creatures. But if these were the defining elements of human experience, we would have perished as a species long ago.[7]

We have seen and continue to see the development of human civilization in people caring for one another. Consider the rise of efforts like CaringBridge, an organization that creates free personalized web pages for people facing medical conditions, hospitalization, and medical treatments. These web pages offer valuable information to family members and friends. Their website's more than fifty million visitors are a tribute to the care people have for one another. You also see this care when tragedy strikes. Millions join every year to care for people in countries other than their own to help survivors of natural devastation, wars, and attacks.

Some work hard to make the ability to cross to the other side in acts of empathy even more possible. Mary Gordon of Roots of Empathy, a classroom-based program to build caring, peaceful, and civil societies through the development of empathy in children and adults, says that "empathy is the ultimate human trait. The ability to understand the other. It is the connective tissue to our shared humanity."[8]

Another program, Start Empathy, also focuses on schools. They provide a starter kit for classrooms to begin the work of making changemakers in the world. They are part of the Changemaker Schools Network, a global community of leading elementary, middle, and high schools that prioritize empathy, teamwork, leadership, problem solving, and change making as student outcomes.

Eric Dawson does this work through Peace First, whose global goal is "to increase global empathy" with school-aged people. They have created an inspiring manifesto that begins, "The world is a harsh place. People are treated unfairly. People are scared. People get hurt. This matters because people matter. All people. I know I can't be perfect. I know I cannot fix everything. But I can make a choice. I can choose to be a peacemaker. And I commit to making this choice, every day." The group's website shares stories from the more than forty thousand children around the world whom they have trained to be empathic changemakers.

"There is a greater miracle than walking on water," Thich Nhat Hanh wrote. "It is walking on earth for peace."[9] And this Buddhist master spiritual guide and philosopher is among others who have created a movement of global empathy, capturing Jesus's teaching of "they will do even greater works than these."

PARTICIPATION

That Time with the Spit and the Mud

As Jesus walked along, he saw a man who was blind from birth. Jesus' disciples asked, "Rabbi, who sinned so that he was born blind, this man or his parents?"

Jesus answered, "Neither he nor his parents. This happened so that God's mighty works might be displayed in him. While it's daytime, we must do the works of him who sent me. Night is coming when no one can work. While I am in the world, I am the light of the world." After he said this, he spit on the ground, made mud with the saliva, and smeared the mud on the man's eyes. Jesus said to him, "Go, wash in the pool of Siloam" (this word means *sent*). So the man went away and washed. When he returned, he could see.

John 9:1–7

The story of a man receiving his sight after Jesus applies a mudpack made from the dust of the road and his own spittle is one of the most memorable and significant stories in all of the Bible. While it's the story of a man gaining the ability to see with his eyes, it is also the story of people acquiring the capacity to perceive and see in new ways. And it's a story calling humanity to the path of helping people to bring about sight and understanding.

This story has long been one of my favorites. It was one of the first stories I remember reading when I started in my Christian faith as a sixteen-year-old. Right from the start of my faith, this story captured my imagination. I have thought about, told and retold, read and imagined the scenes in this story countless times. I have choreographed the movements, characters, and even emotions of this story in my mind's eye so often that I almost feel like I actually saw it happen.

My Imaginative Telling

For me, this story begins with a dusty, crowded, bustling road. The road runs into, and out of, a portal in the outer walls of

Solomon's temple, in the heart of Jerusalem. The temple is not only the religious center of the city, and of many people's faith, but also a center of commerce. The outer area of the temple is public space where the religiously observant, the unclean, the nonbeliever, and the gentile gather.

This road, however, is just a passageway. People are on this street to go to or come from the temple, where the action is. The only people on this street on purpose are the outcasts and the overlooked. It is peppered with the left-out and left-behind of society and of faith. All manner of those considered unclean, unrecognized, and unimportant make their home on this road. Among them is a man who knows this road well. He was born blind and has learned to navigate his way in the world without the use of his eyes. Having been there a long time, he has a certain cachet on this street, at least among the others who call it home. And he has a prime spot for receiving gifts from the temple visitors.

He is sitting by the side of the road, just far enough from the crush of the crowds to allow people a moment to slow down and catch a glimpse of him. He sits up with bowl in hand, giving passersby a chance to show their generosity. Although his eyes don't work, his eyelids remain open. This creates a stark and arresting image that he can sense causes people to bristle and recoil, so he keeps his face pointing down even as he raises his bowl for money.

He has keenly attuned his hearing, smell, and sense of energy over the years and knows this part of the street exceptionally well. He has felt the pain of being a cultural and religious outcast. He knows, far too well, that people believe his blindness to be a sure sign that he is a sinner. He has heard his entire life how the religious people explain his kind of condition as a result of sin.

He can feel how people look right through him and see only his station in life—blind, middle-aged, abandoned by God and people, needing to live off the generosity of those who care about the less fortunate. The thing is, he doesn't feel less fortunate. He has a keen mind. He understands how people treat one another and what it means to be a son of God. His parents raised him in the Hebrew faith, and he heard the Scriptures read in the temple.

His keen ability to listen allows him to hear more of the conversations on that street than most anyone can imagine. One of the results of being the "unseen" is that people often don't even notice him, and they talk more freely in his presence. He knows that all who walk this street have their own struggles; they feel excluded and let down in their own ways.

He is very familiar with the traveling mystics and teachers with their bands of disciples in Jerusalem. They regularly come in and out of the temple most days, especially on the Sabbath, like today. And there is no shortage of people taking their religious teachings from the temple to the street and freely offering their perspective to all who would listen, including him.

When this group of young men and women makes their way down the street, it gets his attention. It is at this point that he hears someone take up a familiar old refrain, "Where does all the evil in the world come from?" It is one of the favorite questions young disciples like to ask their teachers. He has heard this so many times before. He sympathizes with the young ones who do genuinely believe there is a one-sentence answer to their one-sentence question. And he listens to hear how the teachers will respond.

But this time that same old song of a question is played with a slightly new tune. "Rabbi, who sinned so that he was born blind, this man or his parents?" This time feels different. The question is familiar, but the way it is asked is not. There seems to be a real sense of confusion. It's as if this were the best way the person could phrase his thought, but it's not really what he wanted to ask. This disciple seems to recognize already that this age-old question doesn't fit.

And the blind man knows—he feels—the question is directed elsewhere but asked about him. He can feel eyes upon him. He knows well what it feels like to be treated as a spectacle, an object lesson of sorts. This has happened so many times before.

While the question seems slightly offbeat, the response rattles him. "Neither he nor his parents." He has thought this himself but never heard anyone else say it. "This happened so that God's mighty works might be displayed in him. While it's daytime, we must do the works of him who sent me. Night is coming when no one can work. While I am in the world, I am the light of the world."

This is not the response he had expected. The phrase "so that God's mighty works might be displayed in him" lingers in his mind and repeats like a loop over and over. He considers the rest of the response, and it's just about the point when Jesus says, "I am the light of the world," that he feels the man who is speaking moving toward him.

The blind man recalls hearing the phrase "the light of the world" from the temple, where the first five books of the Hebrew Bible are called the "light to the world." His favorite use of this term is not from the Torah though, it's from the 119th psalm, "Your word is a lamp before my feet and a light for my journey" (v. 105). If anyone understands the longing to have a path made clear as you walk, it's him. So, when he hears this expression, "I am the light of the world," it's something new, fresh, and riveting. Who would say such a thing?

The man notices the crowd getting quieter, and he can feel the man who is speaking moving closer, to now sit next to him. With his head still facing down, he realizes it is no longer possible to be anonymous. He's now part of this group's activity, whatever that is.

The man who is sitting next to him quietly spits on the ground and begins to twirl the saliva and dust to make mud. He hears what is happening, recalling spit and dust from the creation story in Genesis—"*And the LORD God formed man of the dust of the ground, and breathed into his nostrils the breath of life; and man became a living soul*" (Gen. 2:7, KJV).

This use of dust pulls Jesus firmly into the man's story. As one who has spent so much of his life sitting on the ground, the man is well acquainted with dust. He has felt it on his skin, has tried to remove it from his nostrils. Using the very dust that has given him such trouble as part of his healing is a kind of foreshadowing of and commentary on all those disheartening questions about "whose sin . . . ?" being reworked and reapplied as a balm of healing.

Slowly, gently touching the man eyes, Jesus applies the mud. Then quietly he says, "Go, wash in the pool of Siloam."

The blind man knows, of course, that "Siloam" means "sent by God." He is now being sent by God. And he is hurriedly making his way to the pool. Washing the mud from his eyes, he now sees.

Returning to his spot on the street, he sees it in a new way. But the healer and his entourage are gone. In my imagined version of the story, the scene closes with the man looking at the bowl he used for collecting money, saying to himself, "What will I do with this thing now?" He knows that an entirely new path is laid before him.

I really love this story for its passion and grit. Both in my imagined and embellished version and in its 139-word Gospel of John version.

Even without my dramatic telling, this is, for good reason, one of the more famous stories of the miraculous signs of Jesus. Not only because of its spectacular features—a man born blind who is suddenly able to see; a healing paste created from spit and dirt; a traveling prophet bringing healing to a man who never asked for it—but also because of four unique features of this story that give great insight into the "do even greater works" nature of this sign.

An Afterword

It takes the remainder of John 9 to tell the whole story. The story goes into detail about the personal, religious, and family ramifications of this healing.[1] None of the other signs so far have allowed the reader into the implications of the miraculous sign. As the afterword rolls out, we see the depth of attitude about the man and Jesus. The conflict centers not only on what

Jesus did but on the fact that he did it on the Sabbath. For this, both the man and Jesus are condemned.

In this afterword we meet the man coming to understand that it was Jesus who made the mud and invited him to wash at the pool. Like the other signs we've read about, there is an anonymous quality to this story. This healing is not contingent on the man holding any particular opinion about or belief in Jesus.

Jesus Gives an Explanation of
What He Is Doing before He Does It

In the other miraculous signs, there is minimal conversation about the events. And there is certainly no commentary from Jesus about what is happening. But this story is framed as question-response-action right from the start. When he's asked who sinned, Jesus doesn't even bother debating between the two options, the man or his parents. Rather, Jesus shifts from a punishment-of-sin narrative to explaining that we can see the mighty works of God in all people. Jesus's use of the phrase "This happened so that God's mighty works might be displayed in him" anticipates the kinds of phrases Jesus uses about himself in John 10, the very next chapter, to argue that he was sent from God. In some ways this is an afterword to the afterword—John 10 provides deeper understanding of how Jesus is using the notion of "the works."

This dialogue comes as the commitment to have Jesus executed is building among the religious establishment:

Again the Jewish opposition picked up stones to stone him. Jesus responded, "I have shown you many good works from the Father. For which of those works do you stone me?"

The Jewish opposition answered, "We don't stone you for a good work but for insulting God. You are human, yet you make yourself out to be God."

Jesus replied, "Isn't it written in your Law, 'I have said, you are gods?' Scripture calls those to whom God's word came gods, and scripture can't be abolished. So how can you say that the one whom the Father has made holy and sent into the world insults God because he said, 'I am God's Son'? If I don't do the works of my Father, don't believe me. But if I do them, and you don't believe me, believe the works so that you can know and recognize that the Father is in me and I am in the Father." (John 10:33–38)

Jesus flips the narrative around, presenting the man as one who displays the works of God, as a son of God, not as an object lesson for a debate about sin. The works of God are evidence of someone being part of God's family, God's son in this case: "Believe the works so that you can know and recognize that the Father is in me and I am in the Father." What is the author of the gospel doing with this story? This blind man, who in the eyes of the religious and cultural systems of the day was an outcast on the wrong side of sin, is now elevated by Jesus to be the very partner of God in showing the works of God.

The disciples receive a new vision of humanity to apply to their categories and assumptions even before the man gets new vision with his eyes. This is a sign showing humanity new ways to see and understand one another.

A Two-Part Participatory Sign

Another unique and crucial feature of this sign is that it's the only one that takes place in two parts. Jesus touching the man's eyes is part one. But that doesn't allow the man to see. The seeing comes in the second part when the man goes to the pool to wash. Jesus doesn't speak to the man until he gives him the invitation to wash in the pool. This miracle is a participatory act between the man, Jesus, and the pool. Zoom in on that participatory nature. Giving sight is not something one does for the other. It is something people participate in together. The man is portrayed not merely as being in need. He is a coconspirator in his healing.

This One Includes Touch

This is the only miraculous sign in John's Gospel in which Jesus touches the person. In all the others the miracles were performed through Jesus's words. In this case, when he does touch the man, it is only the start of the miracle; the miracle is completed later. It takes the pool washing for healing to take place. It is almost as if the Gospel of John wants to make the point that these miraculous signs are not limited to Jesus's body being present. His touch is not the necessary component.

In this story, however, Jesus does touch. And he gets really close when he touches him, right in the man's face. He gets down and dirty, literally, as he makes mud from his spit. The specifics of this touch-miracle are intentionally set as a response to the disciples' question about who sinned. Not only did Jesus touch him, but he touched him on the part of his body where the "sin" was manifest—his eyes. This touch connects Jesus with the man. Jesus is not looking through him, seeing only his condition. He is looking right into the man's eyes, even though the man can't see back, yet.

Jesus sees the man long before the man sees Jesus. This is a lesson for all of us in how to connect with another's humanity. We are to pull close to others, even to those we have been told are the problem or the most hopeless. The man born blind is the very tapestry in which the works of God are displayed. That should reassure us that all hope is never lost.

Those Doing This Work by Bringing Sight to Eyes and Minds

All the qualities of this incredible story help to show the way humanity can and is working to bring about sight, to increase our capacity to see people. Just as both the man who couldn't see with his eyes and the people who are blinded by their biases are given vision in this story, so also this is work being done across the world.

People are participating in this miraculous sign today in both the way the disciples saw humanity anew and the way the man was able to see. Just as the disciples needed to change the way they saw the world, so do we need to see differently in our world. Seeing, recognizing, and understanding are as much work of the mind as of the eyes. People are doing the vital job to help humanity see one another—past those deep mental blocks that keep us from really seeing.

Christopher Chabris and Daniel Simons study perception and attention, and they have shown how common it is for people not to register mentally what their eyes take in. I have used their video "The Invisible Gorilla: How Our Intuitions Deceive Us" dozens of times with groups, and every time I am amazed by what happens.

The video is of six people passing two basketballs around. Three of the people are wearing white shirts, and three are wearing black shirts. The people in the two groups weave around one another, the three in white shirts passing one ball among themselves and the three in black shirts passing another ball among themselves. I instruct the viewers to silently count how many times the people in white shirts pass the ball to each other. The clip lasts just over one minute.

About twenty seconds into the video, after the people wearing the white shirts have passed the ball nine times or so, a person in a black gorilla suit walks into the picture from the right and stands in the middle of the room. The gorilla faces the camera, points at himself with his thumbs, and does a little dance before exiting to the left. The gorilla is on the screen for nine seconds, during which the six people continue to weave around, passing the two balls.

At the end of the video, I ask people how many times the white shirts passed the ball to each other. I ask, "How many counted fourteen times?" Hands go up. I go on, "Fifteen, sixteen, seventeen, eighteen, nineteen?" Hands go up for all these numbers. Then I ask, "How many people saw the gorilla?" There is often a chuckle at the question. Almost every time I do this, fewer than half the people in the room indicate they saw the gorilla. This brings laughter from those who saw and confusion among those who did not. I ask those who saw the gorilla to tell those who didn't what they saw. The looks on people's faces are precious. Then I show the video again. This time, everyone sees the gorilla, and the room fills with laughter and disbelief as people wonder how they missed something so obvious the first time around.

Chabris and Simons say the reason people don't see the gorilla is not that something is wrong with their eyes. Their eyes take in the light photons just fine. They do see the shape of the gorilla, but they do not recognize it as meaningful.

This makes sense. The instructions were to pay attention to the people in white shirts, so the viewers unintentionally ignored the people in black shirts, and this meant the gorilla was also ignored. So while their eyes registered the presence of the gorilla, their brains determined that it wasn't relevant to the task at hand and let the information go.

Interestingly, the people who don't see the gorilla usually get correct the number of passes among the white shirts. They were paying attention to what they were told was essential, and they fulfilled the duty assigned to them.

Chabris and Simons have many such experiments focused on what they call the "illusion of attention." They explained to me that rather than this being an occasional act, it's the way most of us function all the time. Mostly, that's a good thing. There are far too many stimuli around us for us to pay attention to all of them. We can't notice every bird or sound or heartbeat or idea—our brains would get overwhelmed. So we have evolved in a way that allows us to organize our lives by a subconscious set of priorities.

Chabris and Simons call this our "attention set." An attention set is that which you already know to be true or obvious; it then directs your attention. For example, they studied sixty-two accidents in which a car struck a motorcycle. The accidents had something interesting in common: none of the car drivers had a motorcycle license. Their conclusion? What helps people see motorcycles is not bumper stickers that demand "Start Seeing Motorcycles." It is having personal experience riding motorcycles.

The authors said these attention experiments reveal two things: we are missing a lot of what goes on around us, and we have no idea how much we are missing. We think we pay attention to far more than we actually do.

It is possible, and in fact quite common, that people either don't see those who are marginalized or only recognize them when they stay in their expected circumstances.

This is a standard dramatic story line in modern-day stories. This is the phenomenon that sits at the heart of the Black Lives Matter movement. There is need to make a particular point to pay attention to realities that our cultural norms and even biases prevent us from seeing. That's one of the compelling aspects of this "attention set" understanding: not all sets are missed due to negligence. Far too often there are deliberate efforts not to see some people or issues.

These efforts are being reversed by those who are demanding that we turn our attention toward people too often ignored or overlooked. Native American activists in North Dakota pushed the nation to listen to them on issues that affect their ancestral lands as it relates to the Dakota Access Pipeline. It took a massive amount of creativity and effort to bring this cause to public consciousness in 2016.

This was vital in the civil rights work in the United States. Consciousness needed changing so people could see and recognize what was happening.

This is at the heart of the current #MeToo movement, where woman are telling their stories of being sexually harassed and abused in our society.

Being seen and counted have brought great healing and some measure of justice for victims of abuse in the Catholic Church.

And there is more good work being done as people care for and love one another around the world. Recently I was talking with a friend whose marriage was, in his words, "on the brink of a painful ending," which was unwanted. He and his wife were separated, and the path to counseling was narrow and rocky at best.

He confided that, three months earlier, his wife had told him she wasn't happy in their marriage and asked him to go to counseling. He told me, "I was a real asshole and said I wouldn't go." After meeting with his therapist, he came to realize that his fear of going to counseling was coming from significant childhood trauma. When his wife had asked him to go to counseling, he said, "It was like a bright light of fear flashed in front of my eyes, and all I could see was my fear and pain. Not her pain and need. I was blind to her and her needs because of my fear."

The therapist who helped my friend see his own pain and see his wife and her situation was a miracle sight-bringer. Therapists, counselors, life coaches, and spiritual directors are doing life-changing work by helping people not only to see others and themselves but also to engage fully in more honest and open ways.

Healing Blindness

The act of seeing with our eyes is, frankly, incredible.

Just pause for a moment and consider what goes into your ability to see anything at all. First, all seeing with our eyes begins with light waves. As light waves come toward your face, some of them are allowed into your eye. The light passes through a thin veil of tears in the front of your eye, which focuses the light to ward your cornea. There the light passes through a liquid called the aqueous humor (which is doing the double duty of focusing light waves and keeping the pressure of your eye constant to maintain its shape). The light keeps moving deeper into your eye, passing through your pupil, which is constantly changing size to control how much light gets through, depending on how close you are to the light.

From there the light is directed to the center of your eye, where it is bathed in moisture from a jelly-like substance called the vitreous humor. The light then reaches the back of your eye and your retina. Your retina is a complex system of blood vessels, nerve endings, photoreceptors, and tissue. These fibers, photoreceptors, and nerves send signals along the optic nerve to the visual center in the back of your brain.

From there your brain interprets the signals, and you "see."

In such a complex system, there are many kinds of loss of sight, and the term "blind" is actually a spectrum. There are many reasons people lose their sight and many ways to help people regain levels of sight function. For millennia people have committed themselves to helping people regain sight and to finding alternative ways for the human brain to interpret impulses so a person can see.

The creation of the Braille system for reading in 1829 by Louis Braille has been an incredible advance in helping visually impaired people read. While it has lost favor in recent decades as new technologies for reading and different philosophical views over how blind children should receive an education have developed, it is an excellent tribute to helping people who cannot see read.

For many children of 1970s, the notion of the "bionic" eye is a riveting image. TV character Steve Austin, of *Six Million Dollar Man* fame, had one. He was a NASA astronaut who was nearly killed in a spacecraft crash, but, as the TV show theme song put it, "We can rebuild him. We have the technology." He was given all kinds of enhancements, including a bionic eye that had 20 to 1 zoom capability. As a ten-year-old, I was impressed not only by the zoom potential but also by the "*ch-ch-ch-ch*" sound effect that went with the zoom. It was so cool that we kids would close one eye and make that sound imagining that we could bionically see. This might be why the Argus II system has been dubbed the "bionic eye." This one is not science fiction. It is for people who suffer from an incurable genetic eye disorder called retinitis pigmentosa. Genetic mutations cause their photoreceptors to stop working and die.

Using the Argus II does not give these people 20 to 1 zoom capability, but it does allow them to distinguish doorways, curbs, and obstacles. And it reengages their brains in the act of seeing, which Dr. Mark Humayun, one of the scientists behind the Argus II, says is one of its significant contributions.

It has a camera and visual processing unit that the patient wears. An antenna on a pair of glasses transmits the data from the camera and visual processing unit to a receiving antenna implanted in the patient. Visual information from the camera mounted in the glasses is converted into an electrical signal the brain can interpret. According to an article on the Business Insider website, "The camera and visual processing unit do what the photoreceptors in people with retinitis pigmentosa no longer can: convert visual information from light into electrical signals the brain can understand."[2]

Echolocation

We know that bats can find their way into their small holes with the use of echolocation. They can catch a bug in midair by sending sound waves out and responding to the bounce back. So, we know that echolocating can be incredibly accurate. For some reason, however, even though I know that bats are mammals and share so much in common with humans, I had assumed that this was a place of distinction.

The ability to "see" your surroundings not by photons entering the iris but by sound waves hitting your eardrum is at first blush simply amazing. As it turns out, the reason we don't use echolocation is not that we can't but that we turned it off.[3]

Studies indicate that sighted and unsighted people can "turn on" their echolocating ability. A YouTube search for "humans using echolocation" will bring up videos of people who are nearly functionally blind walking at incredibly fast paces, playing basketball, rollerblading, and riding bicycles. All this is accomplished by using a refined receptivity to sound waves.

Those who are giving others the opportunity to say, "I was blind, and now I see," whether by creating new perspectives and understanding, by using implanted electrodes, or by using sound waves, are all part of the line of greater works dating back to the man sitting by the side of a road.

LIBERATION

That Time the Dead Guy Didn't Stay That Way

10

A certain man, Lazarus, was ill. He was from Bethany, the village of Mary and her sister Martha. (This was the Mary who anointed the Lord with fragrant oil and wiped his feet with her hair. Her brother Lazarus was ill.) So the sisters sent word to Jesus, saying, "Lord, the one whom you love is ill."

When he heard this, Jesus said, "This illness isn't fatal. It's for the glory of God so that God's Son can be glorified through it." Jesus loved Martha, her sister, and Lazarus. When he heard that Lazarus was ill, he stayed where he was. After two days, he said to his disciples, "Let's return to Judea again."

The disciples replied, "Rabbi, the Jewish opposition wants to stone you, but you want to go back?"

Jesus answered, "Aren't there twelve hours in the day? Whoever walks in the day doesn't stumble because they see the light of the world. But whoever walks in the night does stumble because the light isn't in them."

He continued, "Our friend Lazarus is sleeping, but I am going in order to wake him up."

The disciples said, "Lord, if he's sleeping, he will get well." They thought Jesus meant that Lazarus was in a deep sleep, but Jesus had spoken about Lazarus' death.

Jesus told them plainly, "Lazarus has died. For your sakes, I'm glad I wasn't there so that you can believe. Let's go to him."

Then Thomas (the one called Didymus) said to the other disciples, "Let us go too so that we may die with Jesus."

When Jesus arrived, he found that Lazarus had already been in the tomb for four days. Bethany was a little less than two miles from Jerusalem. Many Jews had come to comfort Martha and Mary after their brother's death. When Martha heard that Jesus was coming, she went to meet him, while Mary remained in the house. Martha said to Jesus, "Lord, if you had been here, my brother wouldn't have died. Even now I know that whatever you ask God, God will give you."

Jesus told her, "Your brother will rise again."

Martha replied, "I know that he will rise in the resurrection on the last day."

Jesus said to her, "I am the resurrection and the life. Whoever believes in me will live, even though they die. Everyone who lives and believes in me will never die. Do you believe this?"

She replied, "Yes, Lord, I believe that you are the Christ, God's Son, the one who is coming into the world."

After she said this, she went and spoke privately to her sister Mary, "The teacher is here and he's calling for you." When Mary heard this, she got up quickly and went to Jesus. He hadn't entered the village but was still in the place where Martha had met him. When the Jews who were comforting Mary in the house saw her get up quickly and leave, they followed her. They assumed she was going to mourn at the tomb.

When Mary arrived where Jesus was and saw him, she fell at his feet and said, "Lord, if you had been here, my brother wouldn't have died."

When Jesus saw her crying and the Jews who had come with her crying also, he was deeply disturbed and troubled. He asked, "Where have you laid him?"

They replied, "Lord, come and see."

Jesus began to cry. The Jews said, "See how much he loved him!" But some of them said, "He healed the eyes of the man born blind. Couldn't he have kept Lazarus from dying?"

Jesus was deeply disturbed again when he came to the tomb. It was a cave, and a stone covered the entrance. Jesus said, "Remove the stone."

Martha, the sister of the dead man, said, "Lord, the smell will be awful! He's been dead four days."

Jesus replied, "Didn't I tell you that if you believe, you will see God's glory?" So they removed the stone. Jesus looked up and said, "Father, thank you for hearing me. I know you always hear me. I say this for the benefit of the crowd standing here so that they will believe that you sent me."

Having said this, Jesus shouted with a loud voice, "Lazarus, come out!" The dead man came out, his feet bound and his hands tied, and his face covered with a cloth. Jesus said to them, "Untie him and let him go."

Therefore, many of the Jews who came with Mary and saw what Jesus did believed in him. But some of them went to the Pharisees and told them what Jesus had done.

John 11:1–46

The seventh and final miraculous sign Jesus performs in the Gospel of John is a real doozy. Jesus calling Lazarus from the grave and Lazarus stepping out of the tomb is by far the most dramatic and impressive of all the miraculous signs. It is also one of the more difficult stories to get our minds around. We will likely find that it is the most complex of the seven, both in its structure and in how we are called to do and outdo this work.

This miraculous sign is different from the others on many fronts, from the content to the form to the meaning. We will use the pattern we have applied for the others, but we will have to flex some new miracle insight muscles. This is in part due to the length of the story. It is a long text. The other miraculous signs recorded are considerably shorter; water to wine, two hundred words; healing the son with the fever, two hundred; the man at the pool, just under three hundred; walking on water, about two hundred; loaves and fishes, just over three hundred. This one clocks in at over a thousand words!

It is not only long; it is also structured differently than the previous stories. This story spans five days, involves two sets of necessary dialogues, and in a genius way takes the reader into new understandings of familiar ideas. The content of the story itself asks us to look past our assumptions to see what is going on with this sign. A dead man coming back to life and returning home to make a meal (see John 12) is the kind of story that is well outside the norm, even compared to the other signs in the gospel.

If any of the miraculous signs were going to put the "doing greater things than these" notion through its paces, this one is certainly it. While I was talking about the ideas in this book to a group recently, one man skeptical about the "do greater things" notion said, "Say what you want about people doing what Jesus did, but no one I know has brought a person four-days dead back from the grave. That is something only Jesus did."

Good point.

At first blush, this story seems the least likely for repeatability. I've never heard of anyone even giving it much of a try. Very few people head into a funeral preparing to pull a person from the casket with a shouted invitation or even a helping hand. This is not the kind of story people have taken as their organizational namesake, as they have for the feeding of the five thousand.

Frankly, if this story were the tipping point in any assessment of the reasonableness of the stories of Jesus, I wouldn't blame people for calling them unreasonable. And when I came to this story, I was nervous about how to approach it from the "greater things than these" angle. It is such an odd and over-the-top story, it's hard enough to believe at any level, let alone to suggest that we should do or outdo it.

Like the other miraculous signs, this one points humanity to a way of valuing life in the here and now and not allowing any belief to keep us from doing all we can to seek life and keep hope alive. If this story were intended to call people to find a way to beat death, I would write about cryonics or the fantastic advances in medicine that someday may allow cryopreserved people to be revived. Or I would tell about the incredible life-saving support systems in hospitals that keep people's bodies functioning until a cure or intervention can be found. We would spend time discussing the "Lazarus effect," in which people come back to life as long as forty minutes after being pronounced deceased.[1] I would gladly extol the life-saving power of defibrillators and mouth-to-mouth resuscitation and the millions of people who have been revived by these means. But none of those gets at what this miraculous sign is pointing to. This story is about something more significant.

Only in the Gospel of John, Really?

It is vital as we consider this sign to remember that the Gospel of John has crafted an overarching narrative in a specific way to call people to a way of life. This story is told in service of that message. While all the miraculous signs we have looked at are only in John and not in the other gospels, that fact is particularly notable in this case because it is so blatant and troubling that the other gospels don't include it.

The other gospels include stories that seem similar to the ones in John. They tell of healings of men's legs and eyes; they have different versions of the feeding of thousands and walking-on-water stories; a young boy with a connection to a Roman soldier is healed in them. But there is nothing like the Lazarus story in Matthew, Mark, or Luke. Because of the significance of the content of this story, that is more than a bit shocking.

It is also odd that the names of the people in this story are used in the other gospels. But those gospels tell entirely different stories about these people. The Gospel of Luke includes stories about two sisters named Mary and Martha. Jesus even goes to their house, but there is no mention of a brother at all, let alone one named Lazarus. There is also no mention of death or illness connected with them.

The Gospel of Luke does include a Lazarus, but he is a character in a parable, not the brother of Mary and Martha, and he is not a friend of Jesus. The parable Jesus tells is about a man named Lazarus who, after death, wants to return to warn his family of the futility of his life but can't cross from death to life. The point of the parable is that there is no going back to the place of the living.

What does all this mean for us as we engage in this story? We should see this story as a stand-alone in the Gospel of John that functions as part of its narrative of all people living in the way of Jesus as the Christ and having life in that way. This story is not primarily about the afterlife or physical deterioration or bringing an end to death. This story calls the people of the Jesus way to have a different understanding and to hope in the here and now.

This Story Might Not Be about What You Think It's About

Resurrection sits at the heart of this story but in a unique way. The story seeks to offer to the characters in the first century, and to us in the twenty-first century, a fresh approach to the topic. This might strike you as odd at first, but this is not a story about "the resurrection of Lazarus." I wouldn't blame you for thinking it is, since it does involve a death-to-life move and Jesus using the phrase "I am the resurrection." I certainly have referred to it that way in the past. Many Bibles even put "The Resurrection of Lazarus" as a header to the text.

But it is not a resurrection story at all, at least not in the Jewish and Christian sense of the word. We will look more closely at what the understanding of resurrection was in the first century, how the "I am the resurrection" phrase frames the point of this story, and why it is important for us to see this as a nonresurrection story. "The raising of Lazarus" serves as a much better title, so I will be referring to the story as such as we make our way through it.

This miraculous sign has many unique qualities. For starters, it is the only one where Jesus is personally and emotionally invested prior to the action. It is the only one where it is publicly obvious who made the miraculous sign happen. It is the only one that spans multiple days. And it is the only one where the meaning of the miraculous sign is declared ahead of time in two conversations with others (which turn out to be very helpful for us).

Conversation One: Jesus and the Disciples

The first conversation is an interaction between Jesus and his disciples. In reading it, you feel like you're on a curvy path, with its talk of life, death, and sleep. The story starts with Jesus getting word that his friend Lazarus is sick and that his sisters want Jesus to come and heal their brother. Right from the start, the story line does not follow a straight, literal path. Jesus's response to the news about Lazarus isn't action but a teaching: "This illness isn't fatal. It's for the glory of God so that God's Son can be glorified through it." As readers of the story, we know that Lazarus is indeed going die, but Jesus seems emphatic that there is something else going on. He uses the term "fatal" in a particular way. For Jesus, this is not a simple "man dies and needs to be revived" event.

After receiving the news, Jesus intentionally waits two days before going to Lazarus's town. In those intervening days, Lazarus dies. Martha, Lazarus's sister, laments that if Jesus had come right away, he could have healed her brother. Jesus's waiting makes him culpable in the death—at least in the minds of his sister.

This story, from its very start, is about more than preventing death. It is about the integration of death and life. Throughout the conversation, life and death do not oppose one another but are found in one another. Yes, saving a life is important, not because life is distinct from death but because death is part of life. Jesus will return to this theme through the remainder of the Gospel of John, right through his own death and resurrection.

After two days Jesus tells his disciples that they need to go to Lazarus's town, which raises the theme of death and life again. This time the issue is not only Lazarus's death is the issue, however, but also the risk such a trip would present to Jesus. His disciples plead with him not to go; they believe it is too dangerous because people in that area want to kill him. Jesus says something about walking in the daytime: "Aren't there twelve hours in the day? Whoever walks in the day doesn't stumble because they see the light of the world." While this may seem cryptic, it is at the heart of this entire story. It is a call to life "now, not later"; it is about urgency and not putting off the work that needs to be done for any reason, even the fear of death.

The dialogue intensifies around the themes of death, sleep, and life. Jesus, in what serves to convince the disciples that there is something more going on here than his survival, says, "Our friend Lazarus is sleeping, but I am going in order to wake him up." As might be expected, this use of "sleeping" raises questions from the disciples: Why does he use such veiled and confusing terms? What is he trying to say? "If he is sleeping, he will get well," they retort.

Jesus flips it around yet again: "Lazarus has died. For your sakes, I'm glad I wasn't there so that you can believe. Let's go to him."

The reader feels the confusion in the disciples. We can almost hear their internal questioning: "What is going on? When did his illness turn to death? Is he sleeping or is he dead? Why is Jesus glad that he wasn't there to save Lazarus? Why are we going—isn't it too late? Why is Jesus going at all—does he have a death wish?"

Thomas's sense of confusion seems to come out as he gives his own interpretation of the situation, that this is not only about the death of Lazarus but also about Jesus, and even the deaths of the disciples. He says, "Let us go too so that we may die with Jesus."

At this point, it's not clear who is living, who is dying, who is sleeping, or who knows what!

That might well be the point of the story. This is a turn-around story of what we think gives us life. This kind of confusion matches what so many people experience around death. The stress, misunderstanding, and meaning of it all are so common when we engage with death. Death is inevitable for all of us. We all know it is coming. And yet, it can render us confused and bewildered.

Conversation Two: The Sisters

After a multiple-day journey, Jesus stops outside the town of Bethany, where Lazarus's grieving sister Martha meets him. The scene is quite dramatic and brings us the second, and more important, conversation in the story.

Martha is not happy with him. "Lord, if you had been here, my brother wouldn't have died," she begins. Her frustration is palpable. She is sure that Jesus could have done something about this illness of her brother's. Presumably, she knew about all the other signs of healing Jesus had done. Why hadn't he come to heal her brother? Now she is sure it was too late.

She goes on, "Even now I know that whatever you ask God, God will give you." She shows how deeply she believes that he could have done something. She's sure he had, and still has, the ability to help. But he didn't use that ability to help. He didn't do anything, and her hope expired. I think this is why she goes to meet him outside of town. It was a way of saying, "There is no need for you to come now. You could have come before when he was still alive. When hope was alive. But now it is too late."

Many of us know the pain of Martha's "it is too late." We have had our own experience of "If . . . then there would have been hope." We are drawn into the experience of the despair that comes with accepting a situation and realizing that things are not the way we thought they would be. She thought there would be healing for her brother; she even sent word to Jesus about it. She believed something could have been done, but now she lives in the reality of it not happening. She is the realist in this story. She is the one who knows how it is; but it is too late, and nothing can be done now.

So, when Jesus responds to her "if you had been here" lament with "Your brother will rise again," Martha hears this as an unwanted reassurance of a promise that things will be better in the afterlife. That's not what she wants to hear. Anyone who's felt the pain of loss knows that promises about the future can ring like discordant, hollow platitudes. We miss our loved one here, now.

Martha doesn't want an afterlife story, she wants a different life story. As we will see, this is what Jesus wants too.

Martha replies, in what I imagine was a resigned tone, "I know that he will rise in the resurrection on the last day." Here it becomes clear that Jesus was not offering her a "things will be better later" cliché with his "your brother will rise again" statement; instead he was suggesting an alternative to that very understanding.

Jesus replies to Martha's comment with a phrase that might seem very familiar to some of us but was extremely provocative in this story: "I am the resurrection and the life. Whoever believes in me will live, even though they die. Everyone who lives and believes in me will never die. Do you believe this?"

Jesus's use of "I am the resurrection" pulls on her thread of understanding, intending to unravel the notion of the "resurrection on the last day." It might seem subtle, but for those who held to the notion of the "resurrection on the last day," the use of "I am the resurrection" was mind-blowing. Jesus was not reinforcing the "rise on the last day" story line. He was presenting an alternative to it. He was putting together the "living and dying" in the here and now; he was not asking Martha to wait.

The provocative meaning and power of Jesus's statement are rooted in the contrast of the "rise in the here and now" and the "rise again on the last day" visions. Stick with me here, as we look at the first-century notion of "rising on the last day" to understand why the invitational good news in Jesus's "I am the resurrection" is an alternative belief.

"Rise on the Last Day"

The "on the last day" view Martha held was common in her time and has endured to the point that it may even be familiar to many of us. Some in the Jewish community were very committed to the Hebrew belief in *tehiyyat ha-metim* (resurrection of the dead).[2] It marked the end of time when all the righteous would be brought to life in Jerusalem.

Resurrection was a controversial idea in the first century, even among the most religiously devout. Some people rejected it altogether. The Sadducees were famous for arguing that there is no resurrection from the dead, and according to the Gospel of Mark, they were even defined by this view. Mark introduces them as follows: "Sadducees, who deny that there is a resurrection" (Mark 12:18).

First-century Judaism was not alone in its debate about the end of time when the righteous would be brought back. Many religions and systems of thought carry a notion of a future promise even today, be it "life in heaven," "reincarnation," "merging with the universe," or "receiving new bodies on this earth or another planet."

Any view that calls on us to wait for the "last days" is in jeopardy of promoting inaction and prioritizing the future over the now. We have all heard of people putting off caring for people's physical, emotional, and spiritual needs now under the guise of "waiting for heaven," or not interfering with a person's karmic path because it will lead the person to future refinement or some other calculation built on a commitment to a coming reckoning.

Jesus's message was of the "your will be done on earth" variety, not the "wait until another time and another place to make the world right" view. And this was what was going on with the "Work while it is daylight" comment, where Jesus explains why he should be healing on the Sabbath. Jesus was saying that nothing, neither the Sabbath nor the resurrection on the last day, should keep us from doing all we can right now to benefit people. ("Sabbath was made for humans, not humans for the Sabbath," Jesus was fond of saying.) There is an urgency to life, we see in his words and actions. There is a right here, right now calling to life.

So when Jesus says to Martha, "I am the resurrection and the life. Whoever believes in me will live, even though they die. Everyone who lives and believes in me will never die. Do you believe this?" he was seeking to replace the notion of "he will rise in the resurrection on the last day."

I Am

Jesus's use of "I am" here shows an urgency that is not about being panicked or in a hurry. It is an urgency born from the very essence of God's constant presence. Recall how Jesus's use of the phrase "I am" is key to seeing what Jesus is doing. Jesus is intentionally calling upon a phrase that would have had great significance to the first-century reader. He uses the "I am" structure six other times in the Gospel of John: "I am the good shepherd," "I am the door," "I am the bread of life," "I am the way, the truth, and the life," "I am the light of the world," and "I am the vine."

The "I am" was powerful in the Jewish community and sits at the heart of Jesus's understanding of God and humanity.

"I am" is the closest thing to a name for God in the Hebrew Bible. Ironically, it is used to avoid giving God a name. The idea is that you can only name something that is separate and distinct from all other things; by naming it you are saying it is this thing and not that thing. God, however, is not distinct from anyone or anything, but all that exists is in God. So, there is no name for God. Rather God is all that is.

As we noted earlier, this use of "I am" comes from the book of Exodus, when Moses is called to lead the people out of slavery in Egypt:

> Then the LORD said, "I've clearly seen my people oppressed in Egypt. I've heard their cry of injustice because of their slave masters. I know about their pain. I've come down to rescue them from the Egyptians in order to take them out of that land and bring them to a good and broad land, a land that's full of milk and honey, a place where the Canaanites, the Hittites, the Amorites, the Perizzites, the Hivites, and the Jebusites all live. Now the Israelites' cries of injustice have reached me. I've seen just how much the Egyptians have oppressed them. So get going. I'm sending you to Pharaoh to bring my people, the Israelites, out of Egypt."
>
> But Moses said to God, "Who am I to go to Pharaoh and to bring the Israelites out of Egypt?"
>
> God said, "I'll be with you. And this will show you that I'm the one who sent you. After you bring the peo-

ple out of Egypt, you will come back here and worship God on this mountain."

But Moses said to God, "If I now come to the Israelites and say to them, 'The God of your ancestors has sent me to you,' they are going to ask me, 'What's this God's name?' What am I supposed to say to them?"

God said to Moses, "I Am Who I Am. So say to the Israelites, 'I Am has sent *me to you.*'" (Exod. 3:7–14)

It is fascinating that in the story Moses asks how he should respond when the people want to know the name of the God who is sending him. And the response is not a name but a new understanding of God, "I Am."

The Hebrew phrase *'ehyeh 'asher 'ehyeh* is translated into English as "I Am Who I Am." The English version seems odd to our understanding of sentence structure. We don't tend to use the first-person singular imperfect form, so it rings a bit hollow. To get at the complexities of the word *'ehyeh*, we should look to words like "existence" and "reality." Those words carry the sense of presence. This use of "I am" helps us understand God as full existence. God as reality. The "I Am" holds all things. Then we can see the "I Am Who I Am" as "God is, God was, God will be." Without beginning or end.

So when Jesus says, "I am the resurrection and the life," this is not a statement about himself but about the noncontingent, ever-present, always accessible, right here, right now God.

This is a call to presence, to replace the "sometime, somewhere, somehow" vision of life.

Jesus so often makes the point that the work he is doing is the work that "his Father is doing." Jesus is saying that God is already alive and working now in the world. So he is simply joining what God is doing. It's an intentional replacement of the "will rise in the resurrection on the last day" theology that dominated in the first century and still holds sway today.

Riley Powell, a Christian spiritual teacher, pointed out to me how the structure of the story is designed to call the reader to shift focus away from a future resurrection so we can begin living the fullness of life now, physically and spiritually alive and active in the reality of the "I Am."

Jesus is pulling the "future resurrection" into the present moment. He is talking about an ever-present life in "I Am." So death is not something else but is ever present in life; we "will never die" in that sense.

No Last Days Here

What might not seem evident, until you spend time with it, is what happens in this story: the raising of Lazarus. It is not anything like the "last days resurrection" at all. If Jesus were trying to give a preview of the "last days resurrection," it would be seen as a real failure. Lazarus is not ushered into a new reality. He does not inherit the earth. Instead, he returns to his old life and is going to have to go through death again. In this story, Lazarus goes home, prepares a meal, and hosts a party—he returns to his same old life (John 12). But none of this is seen as a disappointment. There is great celebration around Lazarus. People can find life even in the times when it seems too late. And even in the places where life seems most vacant, like a four-day closed tomb.

It is *life* that is the theme all the way through the Gospel of John. And this story calls us to action and life now. Yes, there are positive aspects to believing that what we are living now is not all there is to live. And it is powerfully important to many people to recognize that our lives have meaning in the larger context of humanity and that God is active in the world well beyond our years.

But the notion of the resurrection in the first century was a complex and contested idea. People in the Jewish community felt and taught differently on this topic. Jesus is not engaging in that specific conversation in this story; rather, he is helping Martha to see, and he thereby shows the way of humanity, that the work of God does not require waiting for some promised last days.

Why All the Weeping?

So if this is a story showing the presence of God, the finding of life in death and death in life, and the hope that comes from life now, why is there such sorrow, even in Jesus? Returning to the story, we read,

> When Jesus saw her crying and the Jews who had come with her crying also, he was deeply disturbed and troubled. He asked, "Where have you laid him?"
> They replied, "Lord, come and see."

Jesus began to cry. The Jews said, "See how much he loved him!" But some of them said, "He healed the eyes of the man born blind. Couldn't he have kept Lazarus from dying?"

Jesus was deeply disturbed again when he came to the tomb. It was a cave, and a stone covered the entrance.

One of the implications of this story is that it makes the full range of emotions appropriate in all situations. We can grieve without being hopeless. We can hope without having to deny the realities of the struggle of life. This story reminds us that in life is death. And in death is life. Death does not bookend life; it inhabits life. We don't have to see our life now, a break during death, and then a returned life on the "last days." That breaks life apart. We can engage with all the realities and remove the false distinctions.

We can live in the midst of both realities at once; that is what we see in Jesus's weeping in the midst of his full understanding of what is going to happen. Jesus is showing that the human spirit can be sorrowful and hopeful together. This is not a paradox; this is fullness. There is "a time to weep and a time to rejoice," as the book of Ecclesiastes puts it.

I know the real, severe impact death has on the human spirit. I've had the heavy responsibility of being with people when they died and have been privileged to interact with the loved ones of the "too soon departed."

I held my own father's thin wrist and felt the final pulse of blood through his body as he passed. I sat with my mother's body waiting for the funeral director to arrive and grieved with my family. I've prayed for an eighteen-year-old who was on life support following a snowmobile accident as his parents requested I make the sign of the cross on his forehead as the hospital staff removed his breathing tubes. I've had my hand in my dying friend's mouth, mistakenly trying to clear his throat, before I realized he was having a heart attack when he collapsed on the basketball court.

I notified a man that his wife and son were killed in a tragic helicopter accident and held him as his legs collapsed under him. I stood in front of people at the funeral of a seventeen-year-old who took his own life and futilely tried to make sense of it for his skeptical and grief-stricken friends and family. I have held the hands of parents who lost children to sudden infant death syndrome (SIDS) and in miscarriages. I am familiar with the devastating power of premature death. It is dark. Horrible. Life-rending.

So I understand Jesus being stricken with the reality of the pain of death and how that led him to weep in sorrow. This story reminds us that any future life does not replace suffering now.

A Prayer and a Call-Out

When Jesus approaches the tomb, he prays. Curiously, in all the miraculous signs in the Gospel of John, this is the only time Jesus prays. At first glance, it is an odd prayer. Jesus indicates that he is saying things for the benefit of those hearing him pray, and it feels as much like a performance piece as a pleading in prayer. "Jesus looked up and said, 'Father, thank you for hearing me. I know you always hear me. I say this for the benefit of the crowd standing here so that they will believe that you sent me.'"

In his recognition of the "I Am," we find the larger frame. He is describing a relational connection like that between a father and a son, one where there is always connection and communication, one where the sent is from the sender. This is a person who is living in the fullness of the life of "I am." "I am" is not so much a name of God as it is a description of the relationship of God to all things. That is at the heart of all Jesus's signs, teachings, and life. Jesus then shouts, "Lazarus, come out!" and the man comes out.

Jesus finishes the miraculous sign by talking not to Lazarus but to those around him. "Untie him and let him go," he says. I love how the story is not over until the people participate in removing the now-unneeded grave bindings and clothes. Can you see the power of this as a story for all humanity? Come out into life. Don't live in the shadows of death. Be freed, be untied from the old story of the grave.

In this story we see people being set free from the stories and expectations that keep us tied up and asleep. Those powers that keep us bound, hidden, and in our graves. This is the work that Jesus calls us to outdo. To free people from their tombs and untie them to live in the fullness of life now.

Saving Lives

There are so many ways that people are standing at proverbial "tombs" calling for people to "come out" and bringing them back from the dead both in body and spirit. Those who do drug rehabilitation work with vulnerable kids on city streets are doing this. Like Peter Jackson, who engages with young men in Chicago every day and impresses on them the value of life even when they see so much death around them. Others saving lives are hospital workers in war zones who are creating settings of life that inhabit places of violence. Work is also being done by those who help people understand the frailty of life and those who ask others to invest their money, time, and passion for meaningful outcomes through charitable giving. They are reminding people that all of life is lived in the midst of death, and they bring significance and meaning to all things.

Possibly the most moving three hours of my life were spent with my friend Shane Claiborne, who asked me to go with him to visit men on death row at Riverbend Maximum Security Prison, twelve miles outside of Nashville, Tennessee. "Yes, count me in," I responded immediately to his invitation.

Nearly as quickly as I said yes, I was struck with fear and heaviness as I considered the significance of this meeting. Up to that point in my life, I had had no personal connection with anyone who was convicted of murder and awaiting execution. I had no idea what I would talk about with the men. I had no idea what I would say if one of them told me he was guilty of killing another person. I didn't know if I wanted to know.

I thought of myself as the kind of person who would look past any man's actions, no matter how grievous, and see him as a full human being loved by God. I sensed this experience was going to call my bluff on this matter. I worried that perhaps "my spirit was willing, but my flesh was weak."

I worried about how I would respond if I met men who maintained their innocence, declaring they were falsely convicted. I knew this was not a hypothetical concern. Four months earlier I had met two men, Derrick Jamison and Anthony Ray Hinton, who were released from death row after spending twenty-two and thirty years, respectively, in prison for crimes they did not commit. I was learning how cruel and unjust the criminal punishment system is in the United States.

I had recently become active in the anti–death penalty movement and began seeing our justice system as deeply flawed. I remain convinced that we should abolish the death penalty for many reasons, including the moral argument that we should not kill people to show that killing people is wrong; the financial argument that capital punishment is far too expensive; the cruel-and-inhumane argument that it is wrong to keep a person alive sitting in a cell only so the state can take the person's life; and the justice argument that far too often innocent people have been executed. I had not only met Derrick and Anthony but also learned that, since 1983, for every nine death row inmates executed, one death row inmate had been exonerated.

I have tried to turn this understanding into action by supporting murder-victim family members and by supporting the conscience of society by working to end the scourge of state-sponsored killing. This has allowed me to meet people who do the vital work of calling for life in the midst of a culture of death: the fine people from Death Penalty Action who provide resources, leadership, and support and who sponsor educational and direct action events and activities within the broader anti–

death penalty movement; the organizers of Journey of Hope . . . from Violence to Healing, a network of murder-victim family members working to abolish the death penalty; people from Amnesty International; and Bryan Stevenson from the Equal Justice Initiative (EJI), which engages lawyers on behalf of the wrongfully convicted and seeks to end mass incarceration in the United States. All these people in their own ways are bringing life to situations that are often filled with a toxic level of pain and grief.

It was through Bryan Stevenson that I had the privilege of meeting Anthony Ray Hinton. Through the work of the Equal Justice Initiative, in 2015 Anthony became the 152nd person exonerated from death row following the presentation of evidence of innocence. Bryan said of Anthony's case, "Race, poverty, inadequate legal assistance, and prosecutorial indifference to innocence conspired to create a textbook example of injustice."

Sitting four feet from Anthony and hearing him tell his story of leaving his cell after three decades, I was reminded of the story of Lazarus. Anthony spoke of how, after sleeping with his knees bent for thirty years because the bunk was too short for his six-foot-three body, he longed to have a large king-sized bed. With tears in his eyes, he shared how even after two years he could only sleep with his knees pulled toward his chest. "I guess it will take a little longer for my mind and emotions to be free. I trust that just as I was set free from the jail cell, I will be set free in my mind as well. But it is apparently going to take some time." The people at EJI are working to "untie him and let him go" with crucial mental health support. There are many tombs in our world that need to be emptied, and that will take all of us, lawyers, law enforcement workers, schoolteachers, artists, activists, and you.

A Long, Harsh Walk

These encounters were fresh as I entered the death row unit of Riverbend Maximum Security Prison in February 2017. I went in with a significant amount of fear and uncertainty, but also with a conviction that the men I would meet had much to show me about life and death. Like so many prisons, Riverbend carries all the markings of a place of punishment. There were armed men and women all around. The concrete walls, the metal cages, the massive sliding doors that echoed with the sound of punishment when they shut—all made for a dehumanizing feel. The entire enterprise is full of pain and misery and is void of life. It was clear to me that this was by design.

It takes a long time to walk through a prison. Moving through secure doorways meant waiting in small hallways for the door behind us to close before the next door would open. I was grateful for the slow passage. I was still nervous about the pending meeting and relished the time to take it all in. We passed men clad in the requisite orange jumpsuits of institutional imprisonment who were living in small cells. It is hard to believe that anyone who understands how restoration or rehabilitation of the human spirit works would create this kind of place.

The death row unit was in a separate building from the main building, so we had to walk outside for one hundred yards or so. Shane, who had been to the facility before, leaned toward me and nodded his head toward a building on our right. "That is the building where they execute the men," he noted with a quiet sadness. My knees nearly buckled thinking that the men would only be allowed outside of these buildings when they were ushered to that building of death.

One of the men we would meet that day, Ron, had his sentence reduced to life in prison and was moved to a different part of the facility a few weeks after our meeting. He sent a note telling about his experience of walking outside. "I saw grass for the first time in 16 years," he wrote. He was not allowed to touch it, of course, but he gushed about the power of seeing green grass and how it filled his life with color and joy, even if briefly.

As we entered the room in the death row building, we were immediately greeted with kindness, warmth, and hugs by ten of the men on death row. My eyes began to water as I took in what was happening. Men on death row, locked inside a maximum security prison, were coming toward me with arms open wide. We immediately started talking in groups of twos and threes around a big table. I'm not sure what I expected, but this was something more welcoming and beautiful than I had imagined. I was impressed with how open and friendly the men were and how much they wanted to talk and engage.

I sat between David and Derrick and was struck by how old the inmates were. Most were in their fifties and sixties. Again, I'm not sure what I expected, but a group of men approaching retirement age was not it. David was fifty-three, just a few years older than me. He told me that he had been on death row since he was nineteen. It struck me that since I was a senior in high school, this man had been held in prison and had not been outside. I tried not to fixate on the fact that in all those years he did not have the freedom to choose how to spend a single day of his life, had not fallen in love, had not made love, had not gone to the grocery store, had not held a puppy or a baby. He had not even stepped on grass. David had not done so many of the things I had done that I felt made my life a life worth living. "How can you live through all this?" I asked him.

With a kind of honesty I had rarely reached myself, he said he made a horrible and wrong choice when he was nineteen years old and had caused much pain to many people. He said, "I am not only what I did at age nineteen, but I am also more than that. I am working on understanding what that is and I am seeking to live in it." As he spoke, I heard the "I am" calling me to Jesus's "I am the resurrection and the life" phrase.

The truth of his statement that he is more than the worse thing he ever did struck me. I thought about how I am such a different person than who I was at age nineteen. I thought about all the people who supported me, loved me, and "called me from the graves" of my choices and helped me "take off the clothes" of my younger self and find a way of freedom and love. I wondered how different this was for David living in this place.

Men with a Death Sentence around a Table of Life

After twenty minutes or so, we pulled the seventeen of us together around the big table. We took plenty of time to introduce ourselves and to tell our stories. The men riveted me. They were so smart, so passionate, so old, so not what my imagination and fears conjured up about death row inmates.

Don, who had been an inmate for over twenty-six years, told us about the table we were meeting around and what made it so meaningful to them. He passionately described how the former chaplain in the prison had invited the men to watch a documentary called *Fambul Tok* (Family Talk). It tells the story of the people of Sierra Leone and how they practiced a long-term process of reconciliation after the genocide between tribes in the 1990s.

That tragic genocide was precipitated and ordered by Charles Taylor, the president of Liberia, in an attempt to overthrow the Sierra Leon government by pitting neighbor against neighbor in acts of murder and cruelty. At the height of the brutality, people were entering one another's homes and killing with machetes and clubs. It was brutal. It was personal. It is a modern-day blot on all of humanity not only for what happened but also for the global lack of action to prevent it.

The documentary describes how, after Taylor's removal, the community sought to rebuild their country and reconcile the lives torn apart by death and violence. They built a massive fire at the center of town, and each night people would meet around the fire and confront one another on the brutality they experienced. "You killed my son," a mother, seeking to be freed from the anger and hatred, would say to a young man. They would talk, cry, engage, reconcile, and search for a way to forgive each other. It is an incredible story in its own right. At the same time, *Fambul Tok* is a modern-day story of people calling one another out of the graves of death, pain, and shame.

Don made it clear how deeply the men on death row at Riverbend understood this story. They knew of this need to be called to life from the midst of death. It compelled them to make their own "Family Talk" space. So they built this giant table. They engraved "Family Talk" in different languages into it. They made the table into a piece of art. And they made it big. There were seventeen of us around it, and there was easily room for another ten. Don told us that for the past five years they have been meeting daily around this table to reconcile with one another and to learn a new way to live. These men who live with death hanging over them, who have childhoods that are among the most brutal imaginable, sit together trying to bring about a new way of life together. As we were saying our good-byes, David looked me in the eyes and said, "Remember us as we meet around this table trying to learn to forgive and love each other. It is really hard to do. We all are in so much pain."

A man with a death sentence on his head meeting around a table with other men seeking a way of forgiveness and life. The connection to the story of Jesus with his friends at the Last Supper before his death was obvious, inspiring, and beautiful to me.

As I left the room with tears in my eyes, I had an impulse to turn and yell, "David, Derrick, Don, Ron, Abu Ali Abdur, Harold, Terry, Kevin, David—come out!" I wanted to say, "Take off their jail clothes and set these men free." But I knew that they were already finding ways to say that to one another every day.

As I walked to the parking lot, my mind turned to the phrase "I am the resurrection and the life. Whoever believes in me will live, even though they die. Everyone who lives and believes in me will never die. Do you believe this?" And I said to myself, "I certainly want to and will do what I can to live like I do."

The raising of Lazarus is in so many ways the ideal way to tell the story of Jesus's call for humanity to be free. Free from the powers that so easily entrap us as individuals and as societies. May we all find the freedom that comes in Jesus's call "to do even greater works than these" as the starting gun for a new way of humanity. May you hear it as a clarion call to join the work, to do the same things, to do even greater things in our day and in our ways as you grow, develop, and extend into greater levels of care, empathy, passion, and love with one another and all living things.

May we all find our Greater Than way in the movement of new humanity, living full, free lives as an ever-expanding benefit and blessing to all the world.

NOTES

CHAPTER 2

1. "Odd Nerdrum," *Wikipedia*, last edited October 26, 2018, https://en.wikipedia.org/wiki/Odd_Nerdrum.

2. Bruce Springsteen, *Born to Run* (New York: Simon & Schuster, 2016), Kindle locations 353–54.

CHAPTER 3

1. "Aiónios," Bible Hub, accessed November 14, 2018, http://biblehub.com/str/greek/166.htm.

2. Jesus also uses a unique title for himself in the Gospel of John, "the Human One" or "Son of Man."

CHAPTER 5

1. Max Roser, "Child Mortality," Our World in Data, accessed November 8, 2018, https://ourworldindata.org/child-mortality/.

2. Sami Yousafzai and Ron Moreau, "The Afghan Village That Saved Navy SEAL Marcus Luttrell," *Daily Beast*, November 8, 2013, http://www.thedailybeast.com/the-afghan-village-that-saved-navy-seal-marcus-luttrell.

CHAPTER 6

1. "Learned Helplessness," *Wikipedia*, last edited October 16, 2018, https://en.wikipedia.org/wiki/Learned_helplessness.

2. Anna Katherine Clemmons, "Training on Hope," *ESPN Magazine*, November 11, 2016, http://www.espn.com/espn/feature/story/_/page/veteranvobora/former-nfl-player-david-vobora-trains-war-veterans-back-brink.

3. "The Artificial Leg Is Invented, November 4, 1846," Library of Congress, accessed November 9, 2018, http://www.americaslibrary.gov/jb/reform/jb_reform_artificial_3.html.

4. Kim M. Norton, "A Brief History of Prosthesis," *Amputee Coalition* 17, no. 7 (November/December 2007), https://www.amputee-coalition.org/resources/a-brief-history-of-prosthetics/.

5. Ananya Bhattacharya, "Paraplegics Are Learning to Walk Again with Virtual Reality," *Quartz*, August 15, 2016, https://qz.com/757516/paraplegics-are-learning-to-walk-again-with-virtual-reality/.

6. Christine E. King, Po T. Wang, Colin M. McCrimmon, Cathy C. Y. Chou, An H. Do, and Zoran Nenadic, "The Feasibility of a Brain-Computer Interface Functional Electrical Stimulation System for the Restoration of Overground Walking after Paraplegia," *Journal of NeuroEngineering and Rehabilitation* #12, no. 80 (2015), https://jneuroengrehab.biomedcentral.com/articles/10.1186/s12984-015-0068-7.

7. Ian Sample, "Paraplegic Man Walks with Own Legs Again," *Guardian*, September 23, 2015, https://www.theguardian.com/science/2015/sep/24/paraplegic-man-walks-with-own-legs-again.

8. Owen J. L. Rackham et al., "A Predictive Computational Framework for Direct Reprogramming between Human Cell Types," *Nature Genetics* 48 (January 18, 2016): 331–35, https://www.nature.com/articles/ng.3487.

CHAPTER 7

1. "Resources for Organising a Food Waste Event," Feedback Global.org, https://feedbackglobal.org/campaign-resources.

2. "Nutrition: Challenges," World Health Organization, 2018, http://www.who.int/nutrition/challenges/en/.

3. Rachel Becker, "World Population Expected to Reach 9.7 Billion by 2050," *National Geographic*, July 31, 2015, https://news.nationalgeographic.com/2015/07/world-population-expected-to-reach-9-7-billion-by-2050/.

4. "World Populations from the Beginnings to the Present," English Online, https://www.english-online.at/geography/world-population/world-population-growth.htm.

5. Jonathan Foley, "A Five-Step Plan to Feed the World," *National Geographic*, accessed November 11, 2018, http://www.nationalgeographic.com/foodfeatures/feeding-9-billion/.

6. Feedback, http://feedbackglobal.org/join-movement/.

7. Feed My Starving Children, accessed November 12, 2018, https://www.fmsc.org/impact-of-our-work.

CHAPTER 8

1. "The Water in You," USGS Water Science School, last modified July 23, 2018, https://water.usgs.gov/edu/propertyyou.html.

2. Kate Shaw, "To Get Parole, Have Your Case Heard Right after Lunch," *Wired*, April 11, 2011, https://www.wired.com/2011/04/judges-mental-fatigue/.

3. Jeremy Rifkin, *The Empathic Civilization: The Race to Global Consciousness in a World in Crisis*, Kindle ed. (London: Penguin Books, 2014), 10.

4. Rifkin, *Empathic Civilization*, 10.

5. "RSA Animate—the Empathic Civilisation," RSA, May 10, 2010, https://www.thersa.org/discover/videos/rsa-animate/2010/05/rsa-animate---the-empathic-civilisation.

6. "RSA Animate—the Empathic Civilisation."

7. Rifkin, *Empathic Civilization*, 10.

8. See the website at http://www.rootsofempathy.org/mary-gordon/.

9. "Thich Nhat Hhan," *Wikipedia*, last edited March 12, 2018, https://en.wikiquote.org/wiki/Thích_Nhất_Hạnh.

CHAPTER 9

1. We will not delve into the afterword in this chapter, but you might find it worthwhile to read John 9 to see the depths of attitude toward the man who was blind. The story brings us back to Jerusalem and puts us, again, near the temple. This proximity to the center of religious power will become important in the prologue to the miraculous sign, when both the man and Jesus are condemned for this miracle again taking place on the Sabbath.

2. Ellie Kincaid, "Here's What Happened When Scientists Gave Blind People a 'Bionic Eye,'" *Business Insider*, July 10, 2015, https://www.businessinsider.com/scientists-put-a-bionic-eye-to-the-test-and-it-helped-blind-people-see-again-2015-7.

3. Damon Rose, "Do Blind People Really Experience Complete Darkness?" *Ouch Blog, BBC*, February 25, 2015, http://www.bbc.com/news/blogs-ouch-31487662.

CHAPTER 10

1. Adam Hoffman, "The Lazarus Phenomenon, Explained: Why Sometimes, the Deceased Are Not Dead, Yet," *Smithsonian*, March 31, 2016, https://www.smithsonianmag.com/science-nature/lazarus-phenomenon-explained-why-sometimes-deceased-are-not-dead-yet-180958613/.

2. "Resurrection of the Dead," *Wikipedia*, last edited September 17, 2018, https://en.wikipedia.org/wiki/Resurrection_of_the_dead#Judaism_and_Samaritanism.